BY DAVID FINKEL

An American Dreamer

Thank You for Your Service

The Good Soldiers

AN AMERICAN DREAMER

AN AMERICAN DREAMER

LIFE IN A DIVIDED COUNTRY

DAVID FINKEL

RANDOM HOUSE

NEW YORK

Published in the United States by
Random House, an imprint and division of
Penguin Random House LLC, New York.

RANDOM HOUSE and the HOUSE colophon are
registered trademarks of Penguin Random House LLC.

Hardback ISBN 978-0-593-59706-4
Ebook ISBN 978-0-593-59708-8

Printed in the United States of America on acid-free paper

randomhousebooks.com

2 4 6 8 9 7 5 3 1

First Edition

Book design by Edwin A. Vazquez

For EHH

AUTHOR'S NOTE

This book is a work of nonfiction journalism based on reporting I did between 2016 and mid-2021 in the United States, primarily in Georgia. I wanted to write a book about being an American in a country becoming ever more divided and combative, and I thought the best way to do that would be to focus on the lives of a small group of interconnected people who spanned the political, racial, and economic spectrums of America and were divided in many ways, but were united in the belief that their beloved country was fracturing. My idea was to document them from Election Day 2016 through Election Day 2020, and that became the basis for this book.

When I began my reporting, I had no way of knowing what would take place in the months and years ahead, only a sense that watching the unfolding story of people wrestling with their own questions about what was happening would lead to a story worth adding to the record of such a pivotal time in American history.

Most of what is described in these pages is based on personal observation, which is the primary source of the reporting I do. All of the people named in this book knew I was a journalist and agreed to participate with the understanding that whatever I heard or saw would be considered on the record.

There are some scenes in the book for which I wasn't present. In those instances, the details, descriptions, and dialogue in this book come from interviews, photographs, videos, court records, contemporaneous emails and text messages, and audio recordings.

AN AMERICAN DREAMER

CHAPTER 1

IT WAS NOVEMBER 3, 2020—Election Day—and soon after Brent Cummings woke up, he called out, "Hey, I'm going to vote."

Who in his big house heard him? He wasn't sure. Probably no one, he realized. His wife, Laura, was already gone. His older daughter, Emily, was away in college, and his younger daughter, Meredith, was asleep in her bedroom. A marriage going on twenty-six years, a twenty-one-year-old daughter, an eighteen-year-old daughter, five bedrooms, four bathrooms, a front porch with a couple of rocking chairs, a large backyard where his daughters had spent hours bouncing on a trampoline in the warming sunshine of Georgia—this was the life Brent Cummings had built since his days as a soldier in the Iraq War, although another way to describe that life was that the trampoline had eventually become covered in leaves and hauled away, his younger daughter who'd been born with Down syndrome had mysteriously stopped speaking, his older daughter was twirling her hair a lot and wringing her hands sometimes and feeling anxious about her future, his wife, normally so upbeat, was spending more and more time fighting off feelings of melancholy, and somewhere in all of this he had become middle-aged.

Out of one war and into another—that was how life in the United States was increasingly feeling to Brent.

The day before, he'd turned fifty-two, and at the end of dinner Laura had brought him a slice of birthday cake.

She was smiling. "I didn't realize till Sunday that there's a difference between white frosting and vanilla frosting," she'd said, and then asked him: "Which do you like?"

"Vanilla," Brent had said.

"Well," Laura had said, "this is white."

He'd taken a bite.

"Yeah," he'd said, "I like vanilla."

He'd slept fitfully, which happened often since he'd come home from Iraq, and when he woke up, he was relieved to have gotten through the night without a bad dream.

He got into his pickup truck. The polling place wasn't far away. He used his turn signals. He didn't exceed the speed limit. He parked between the lines. He opened the entrance door for someone else and let that person go through first. He believed in courtesies and in rules, and he believed that anyone who held doors, didn't lie about cake frosting, didn't cheat, worked hard, and treated people with respect would have a shot at a life of opportunity and meaning.

"Here to vote?" a poll worker asked him.

"Yes sir," he said.

THIRTEEN YEARS EARLIER, Brent had stood in a wide-open field with a few dozen other U.S. Army soldiers, all of them waiting for the rockets that would kill them or the helicopters that would take them out of Iraq. They smoked cigarettes and ground them into the weeds. They talked of the first thing they wanted to do when they got home, and the second thing they wanted to do, and they kept searching the sky. An hour went by. The sun began to set. Another hour went by. There was no telling when the helicopters would show up. That was the best their war could do for them after a year in which dozens of them had been carted away with injuries and fourteen of them had died, and as the survivors kept waiting, a nervous silence descended until one of them said, "They're coming."

It was Brent who had said this.

Everyone had looked toward where he was looking and then had seen them too, a pair of small silhouettes in a big sky lit by a dented-looking moon. The helicopters had come in fast, giving everyone a final coating of Iraqi dust, and then the soldiers were up in the air and on their way home, all of them wondering what was waiting for them in America.

Thirteen years later, Brent had his answer—what had awaited him was this moment on Election Day. In the grand scheme of the day, the vote he was about to cast was the smallest of acts, a mere one vote among what would be one hundred fifty-nine million. And yet as Brent looked at the first name on the ballot, Donald J. Trump, and then the next name, Joseph R. Biden, the moment felt like a reckoning with everything he had been experiencing since he'd gotten on the helicopter and come home to a country that more and more was feeling like it was coming apart at the seams.

He was aware of what people who didn't know him might assume about him, including how he would vote. He'd been born in Mississippi in 1968 and lived there in his formative years, so obviously he was a racist. He'd been raised in New Jersey, where he played center on his high school football team, and then went on to play rugby in college, so of course he was brutish and crude. He had spent twenty-eight years in the U.S. Army and had been in combat, so surely he had killed people. He was a white male pickup-driving ex-soldier living in a Georgia county where in 2016 Donald Trump received 71 percent of the vote, so absolutely . . .

The truth of such assumptions? "It's complicated," Brent sometimes said about all manner of things. He wasn't a brute, although he had once gotten in a fight and hit someone so squarely and with so much force that as his fist kept moving forward, he felt the man's face collapsing bone by bone, a feeling that had sickened him. He wasn't crude, although he was as likely to say the word "fuck" when he was exasperated as the word he wished he would always say, which was "golly." He wasn't racist, he was certain of that, but he wasn't immune to the complications of race, either, not since he was a child who one day climbed into his grandparents' car and began beeping the horn again and again until it got stuck, at which point a black man who worked for his grandfather and was always friendly and patient came over, raised the hood, fixed the horn, lowered the hood, leaned in the window, and whispered so no one else could hear, "You sticks that horns again, I's beat you as black as I is."

The mystery of those words, and the way they made Brent feel, had seared into him and, along with everything else, turned him into the man he had become: probably more Republican than Democrat, probably more conservative than liberal, but most of all a man in the middle, a man who throughout his life had been searching for some sense of larger purpose and meaning. That search had been defining of him, including when he had gone to war talking about the need to be empathetic and honorable, always honorable, with the intention of being the most moral soldier of all.

"Fight over. Congratulations again on a job well done. I'm really proud of you," his father had written to him when he was on his way out of Iraq a year after arriving there. Always, his father had been his guide. In the first hours after his younger daughter Meredith had been born and diagnosed with Down syndrome, when he'd been crying and asking what he was going to do, it was his father who'd given him the answer he'd been trying to live up to since. "Brent, you're going to love her," he'd said. Once again, Brent wanted to believe his father's words, but soon after he got home, he realized that the fight wasn't over, because of a dream he started to have over and over, a bad dream that explained why the election of 2020 had come to mean so much to him.

———

IT WOULD COME, and it would go. But it always came again.

"I haven't had a bad dream in a while," Brent said to Laura one night at dinner.

"In four days," Laura said.

"No," Brent said.

"Yes," Laura said and told him what had happened:

"It's bad! It's bad!" he had cried out.

"Brent, be quiet," she had said, trying to calm him.

"No! It's bad!" he had said.

"Be quiet!" she had said.

She looked at him, waiting for him to finish eating and say something.

One thing about a bad dream for a onetime combat soldier—it could be about so many different things.

A floating body in a billowing shirt, for instance, which some of the soldiers had discovered in the septic tank of an abandoned building they were thinking of moving into. The body was that of an Iraqi. It was toeless and fingerless, and the head was separated and floating nearby, and yet as Brent stood staring at it, the lazy way it was drifting and swirling was kind of hypnotic.

That wasn't the dream, though, and neither was it about the night when the small, isolated base he was on was being bombed and he dove under a truck to take cover. Vehicles were exploding, fuel was leaking from tanker trucks, and fires were breaking out, and as he watched the fires get bigger, it occurred to him that the truck he was under was a fuel tanker and the flames were coming for him.

So the dream could have been about that, or about the early morning mortar that had exploded just outside his room and blown out his window as he slept.

Or it could have been the late afternoon mortar that exploded as he waited in line for his laundry.

It could have been the day toward the end, when he said, "Stupid people. I hate 'em," when everything the soldiers thought they had accomplished in Iraq was falling apart. There were eight hundred soldiers in the Army battalion, and Brent was the second in command. They had spent more than a year trying to bring some stability to an out-of-control area east of Baghdad and thought they'd had some successes. But then came the end, when the school they had gotten up and running was reportedly being stocked with weapons for a final assault on the American soldiers, and the swimming pool they had gotten built, and that just needed to be filled with clean, cool water, was instead filled with twenty armed Iraqi insurgents who had arrived in cars reportedly packed with bombs. Twelve soldiers in Brent's battalion had already died during the deployment, and two more were about to. Seventy others had been badly wounded, a number that was about to go up too, and as Brent monitored video imagery from overhead surveillance cameras, he saw another explosion from another roadside bomb, this one just missing a convoy of soldiers but severing a water main, which created a giant water geyser, which would soon flood part of a town where thirty million American dollars had been spent trying to build a sewer system, which would soften the ground so much the new sewer pipes would collapse. "Glad we're giving these people sewers," Brent said as he watched.

That geyser, and all of the sadness it represented, could have been his dream too, or it could have been what happened a few days later, after the battalion's last two soldiers to die were dead and everyone's hearts were breaking yet again, and the video monitor in the command center showed an armed insurgent firing at a convoy, unaware of the remote camera locked in on him and the .50 caliber machine gun swiveling toward him. "Die, monkey, die," Brent began screaming, and everyone else began screaming it, too, and soon the insurgent was dead, and soon after that, his war over, Brent was on the last helicopter out, skimming across the rooftops of Baghdad and on his way home to America and his dream.

The thing was, everyone went home to some kind of bad dream. As a soldier named Aieti had said once, "There's no way of stopping dreams. If there's a pill that would stop dreams, I'd take it right now."

What were Aieti's dreams, Brent sometimes thought. Or what were the dreams of a soldier named Prestley, who used to say to Brent after an especially bad day, "Fuck it, sir. Let's go eat," and on his last day, as he waited for the helicopter, said, "You know what I love? Baby carrots. Baby carrots and ranch dressing. I think I'm going to be eating some baby carrots when I get home." He had been so happy to be getting out alive. They all had been. Brent, too, although sometimes his happiness wasn't as apparent as with others. "He can see despair" was how

Brent's commander once described him, but Brent saw it differently, as part of his desire to be decent. It was seeing the need, for example, to somehow fish that floating Iraqi body in the billowing shirt out of that fetid water because, as he'd said at the time to another soldier, "I would hope someone would do the same for my body. And for any human being."

Because: "Otherwise, we're not human," he had said.

A few months after that, he was home, having his dream for the first time.

It woke him up. He could feel his heart beating in his throat. He tried to catch his breath.

The dream was of darkness. No, more than darkness. Blackness. It had been from his point of view, and all that he could see was a kind of blackness he'd never seen before. He could tell it wasn't just a color but that it was dimensional. It was below him, above him, and all around him, and it stretched on and on without interruption, accompanied only by the faintest of sounds, a chorus of quiet laughter coming from thousands of people he couldn't see.

They were laughing at him. He understood that, and he understood why, that it was because he was naïve enough and foolish enough to believe his life should have purpose and meaning.

Mocking laughter and blackness into infinity. Worst of all, it felt like the blackness was filled with magnets, trying to pull him in.

That was his dream.

He had never told anyone the details of it, not even Laura, and now, sitting at the table with her as she waited for him to finish eating and say something, he wasn't about to start. Instead, he reminded her of what she used to do when he had trouble sleeping.

"It used to be hugs," he said.

"Shut up," she said, laughing.

IT WAS FALL 2017 at that point, the 2020 election was still far away, and they were at their kitchen table. The house had a dining room they rarely ate in and a living room they used less often than that. They were kitchen-table people who ate dinner at five-thirty in their big house in their beautiful neighborhood in Georgia's most affluent county, where the weekly paper's big story, stripped across the top of the front page, boasted that the county had just been named Georgia's "healthiest for seventh year."

"Pleasantville" was what their next-door neighbor called the neighborhood.

"Mer?" Laura said now, calling to Meredith, who was upstairs.

Earlier, when Brent had passed by her closed door, he'd thought he heard her crying, which had surprised him. Fourteen years old now, she almost never cried, not from emotions, and not from physical pain, either, but she was missing Emily, who a few days before had left for her first year of college. All of them were missing her. She was a brilliant girl, and a beautiful girl, and a shy girl who was missing them, too.

"Why don't people like me?" Emily had just texted them.

She was in her dorm room, waiting to find out if she was going to be invited to join any of the sororities she had applied to as a way to get out of her room and find some friends. She wasn't feeling hopeful. Her shyness was being overtaken by insecurities, and as the wait stretched on, Brent was getting more and more upset that a school would sanction what felt to him like a popularity contest before the new students had even found out where to pick up their mail.

"You get so fired up. And angry," Laura said to him. "You look like you're going to punch something."

"Well, you get all tense and everything too," he said.

"I know, but I don't get angry."

"I feel like sometimes we stepped in dog shit," he said, trying to find a way to explain the moods he fell into, "and it's like you can *not* step in dog shit, you know? Let's steer clear of the dog shit. Let's not get it on our shoes."

There was silence as Laura took that in.

"Okay, but at the same time this was something she wanted to do," she said. "She has no friends. It was something to do."

"I just feel like I could have coached her better," Brent said.

"Okay, Brent, she's eighteen and she can make her own decisions. You coached her well enough for eighteen years," Laura said. "You have to let her make her own decisions and her own mistakes."

"I know. I know. But still. So what happens if our kid doesn't get picked by any of these stupid sororities today? What's that going to do to her ego?"

"Well, then we have to help her move on. That's where you become a parent. You help her move on from it. Without being angry about it."

"Right. Right. I'm getting spun up. I know I'm getting spun up," Brent said.

"It is what it is. Just accept it. It's not changing, so you getting angry about it is not changing the system," Laura said.

"I'm *not* getting angry. I'm getting *frustrated*. There's a difference," Brent said.

"Not really," Laura said.

They both fell silent again, and for a few seconds the only sound was of the birds in their backyard. One thing about their yard—at times it could sound like every songbird in Pleasantville was living in their trees.

Dinner, dishes, some TV, bed, lights out, and then after about forty-five minutes, as Brent fell asleep, he let out a little scream. More and more, he was doing that, too. He wasn't aware of it, but even if Laura didn't know the specifics of his dream, there were things about him she did know and he didn't. One was the sound of that scream, and another was that ever since Iraq, the more he dreamed, the less he seemed able to laugh at himself, which had been one of the things that had charmed her in the beginning.

She loved him, of that there was no doubt, because how else to explain why their marriage had lasted? They were just so different when they met. She was from Kansas, not Mississippi, and her family didn't have a Bible with a list tucked in the back of ancestors who had fought in wars all the way back to the American Revolution, including for the Confederacy in the Civil War. Her father had been a doctor; Brent's had been a salesman. Her mother never allowed chips or soda in the house unless they were hosting the neighbors for bridge; Brent's mother liked to go to college football games, ring a cowbell, and shout herself just about hoarse. Laura's memories of Christmas: Her family would adopt a needy family for the day to shower with gifts, and if she got anything at all, it might be an orange in her stocking and some clothing. Brent's memories of Christmas: "I got so much."

She had a master's degree in accounting and was a runner who imagined herself marrying a runner, not someone in the military, but then she ended up at some Super Bowl party one year, and there was Brent. He was up in a kind of loft area in the house, looking down, and when he saw Laura, he yelled to her, "Can I get your phone number?" and when she said yes, he yelled, "Go get a pen."

"I should have known right then," Laura would say whenever she told the story. *Get a pen,* he'd said. Not: Can you get a pen? Do you have a pen? But she'd gotten a pen and tossed it up, and it went on from there until here they were, another day under way, still in love with each other and dealing with Brent's mounting frustrations, which on this day concerned their oven.

THERE WERE TWO OVENS, actually, stacked vertically in a wall. He had bought them to replace their old, dying ones, and after they'd been installed, he looked at them and realized they weren't lined up correctly. The bottom one seemed a little off. He got out a tape measure, and sure enough, it was left of center, by maybe a quarter of an inch, so he called the place he bought the ovens from, and they sent out a repairman who said yes, the bottom oven was off but that it was a manufacturing problem, so he called the manufacturer, and they sent out a repairman who looked at the ovens and looked at Brent and said:

"This is a big deal to you?"

"Yeah," Brent said. "It is."

And the repairman kept looking at it and finally said he could understand why because maybe they'd sell the house one day and it was the kind of thing an Indian might notice.

"And I don't mean a Native American," he added.

And Brent thought: What? *What?*

How did getting an oven fixed turn so quickly into that?

And this was an instance where Laura was in absolute agreement because similar things had been happening to her, mundane things that suddenly weren't, as mundane as a trip to the grocery store one day where they were giving out cheese samples.

"What kind of cheese is it?" she'd asked.

"This is white American," the woman working there, who'd just handed a sample to another customer, an Asian woman, had said. And then added: "Like you and me."

Laura had felt so embarrassed. She was sure the other woman had heard. She had wanted to say something, but what?

Brent, on the other hand, had said to the repairman, "Well *I'm* not Indian, and *I* noticed," but that was as unsatisfying in its own way as saying nothing at all.

Maybe Laura was right, that he was getting angrier, but maybe what he was angry about was the country he had spent most of his life defending was being overtaken by something he didn't fully understand.

Patriotic cheese.

Xenophobic ovens.

These were his days now, the days of a moral man in the midst of a moment that felt immoral to him, a man who got into bed every night wondering in silence whether this would be another night for the dream. It was what he was wondering when he went to bed on November 3, 2020, and what he had been wondering four years before, on the previous Election Day, November 8, 2016, when, as he'd gone to sleep, Hillary Rodham Clinton was leading Donald Trump and was about to become the president of the United States.

Lights out.

November 9, 2016.

No dream, he realized with relief as he awakened, turning on the TV.

"What the fuck?"

"What?" Laura had said.

"He fucking won," Brent said.

"Are you fucking kidding me?" she said.

They both stared in disbelief.

"He's our fucking president," he said.

CHAPTER 2

THE FIRST TIME Brent gave much thought to Donald Trump was when he was in high school, driving around New Jersey with his friends Rich and Irene. His car then was an old Volkswagen Beetle with no rear seat, and Rich always sat up front next to Brent, leaving Irene to squat in the back on the seat frame as Brent drove faster and faster along hilly back roads. It was a wonderful time. "Slow down!" Irene would yell every time a bump sent her flying toward the ceiling, and all of them would be laughing, and the radio would be blasting out the Howard Stern show, where the guest sometimes would be Donald Trump bragging about his wine and his steaks and his casino and, of course, sex, lots of sex, the best sex ever.

"He was a buffoon," Brent said. "But we all knew it was a gag. We were all in on the gag."

And now that long-ago buffoon had been elected president, and one of the thoughts Brent had as the news settled in was of his father, the man who did everything right. He had been a salesman. First copiers. Then insurance. Then mining equipment. Then he started a company teaching salespeople to be better salespeople. He got married and stayed married and had three children, of which Brent was the oldest. He called Brent "Hot Rod" for some reason, which Brent really liked. He twirled and jangled his keys a lot, a sound Brent was still hearing as a grown man. Their roots were in Mississippi, and even when they moved north when Brent was eight years old, they would return to Mississippi every summer. There, on his grandparents' farm, Brent would ride dirt bikes and skip stones in pond water and chase cattle and fire off bottle rockets, and when he would return to New Jersey saying "y'all," his friends would be merciless. It was a joyous, safe, upper-middle-class life, and through all of it his father gave Brent a vision of America that became his own. Anything was possible in this vision as long as you did the right thing, and his father always did the right thing, right up to the end, when he was filled with cancer and hours away from dying and opening one more can of Ensure in an effort to make it to another day.

If only Brent could get that last image out of his mind, his father choking his way through that can with a salesman's optimism until he had emptied it, but he could not. His father had been sixty-two years old when he died, and now Donald Trump, a man who did everything wrong, was alive at seventy and being rewarded with the presidency. And what, Brent wondered, was the lesson there?

"You can be bombastic and crude and selfish and still get to fly on *Marine One*? How do you look at that and say that's okay?" Brent said of Trump. "My whole life I've been taught that people like him fail. And he's not failing."

It wasn't Trump's positions on issues that bothered Brent, it was Trump's behavior. His bullying. His vulgarisms. His egotism. His lies. His lack of morals. His incessant, demonizing tweets.

Every time he sent out a tweet, Brent would picture a man in some opulent bedroom, sitting on the edge of a bed in nothing but a shirt, boxer shorts, and black socks, hunched forward and grunting as he typed.

Now that grunter was not only about to be his president, he was also going to become his commander in chief.

Often, because it meant so much to him, Brent would think of the oath he took when he was sworn into the Army and pledged that he would "support and defend the Constitution of the United States against all enemies, foreign and domestic." It was an oath of loyalty to a document rather than a pledge of fealty to a person, and it had been his guide through his twenty-five years in the Army, which had included four commanders in chief. Two had been Republicans and two had been Democrats, and he had willingly followed the orders of all four because as far as he was concerned they believed in supporting and defending the Constitution too. Even on the very worst days in Iraq, when his optimism about his mission was fading, he would remind himself of his oath, and his belief in it kept him going through those worst days to better days, and from better days all the way forward to his current assignment as professor of military science at the University of North Georgia, where he was in charge of the physical, emotional, and ethical development of some seven hundred fifty ROTC cadets.

One day, if Brent did his job well, the best of those cadets would swear that same oath when they joined the Army, but in the meantime, they had another promise to live up to that was displayed on a plaque just outside of the building where the ROTC program was located. "A cadet will not lie, cheat, steal, or tolerate those who do," it read, and while not an oath, it was at the core of the Honor Code that applied to every cadet, including one named Dante Harris, who on the day that Donald Trump won the presidency was realizing he was about to get into very serious trouble.

A few days before, Dante had taken a photograph. He had been in a bathroom in the ROTC building, where one of the program's administrators was standing at a urinal. Much later, that administrator, a retired Army major named Richard Neikirk, would describe what happened to school investigators. "I was wearing a pair of shorts that had no zipper or buttons, so I had to pull the shorts down, along with my underwear," he would say, according to the school's investigative report. "This exposed my backside. A Cadet was in one of the bathroom stalls and when he exited the stall, he took a picture of me urinating with my naked backside exposed. My back was towards him and I never saw the Cadet."

That was the picture Dante took. He took it surreptitiously while standing at a sink, aiming his camera at a mirror. It showed a fifty-nine-year-old man whose buttocks were fully revealed.

Soon after, Dante showed the picture to another cadet,

asking if he wanted to see something funny. The cadet asked Dante to forward it to him, and Dante did.

Then Dante showed it to a few other cadets and sent it to them, and they in turn began forwarding it and posting it to various group chat boards along with messages like, "Do you want to see something fucked up?"

One group had five members. Another group had ten members. Another had twenty. One group made the photograph its avatar. According to the report, one of the cadets would tell investigators that "within 24–36 hours, 'everybody knew about the picture,'" and now, three days after Dante took it, and as Brent drove toward campus wondering what he might say to his cadets about the country's newest commander in chief, Dante went into the dining hall for breakfast, heard people talking about the photograph, saw people looking at the photograph, and understood with a sinking feeling that the photograph was everywhere.

ONE OTHER THING about Dante on that day: He was a twenty-year-old black man, which would figure prominently into what Brent would do when he learned what was going on.

That didn't happen right away. The ROTC program was divided into two staffs. One of them, headed by a civilian who worked for the university and whose title was commandant, handled such things as housing, discipline, records management, and room inspections. Richard Neikirk, whose photo Dante had taken, was the assistant commandant on that staff.

Brent, on the other hand, worked for the Army, not the university. His job was to identify the most promising of the cadets, educate them, enter them into a formal contract with the Army that would bind them to Army careers, and commission them as Army officers when they graduated from college. To that end, he and his staff didn't typically get to really know cadets until their sophomore year in school, when the search began for the next group of cadets to put on contracts.

That was the point Dante had arrived at when Brent first became aware of the photograph. He was going over the list of cadets with Tom Palmer, the commandant, and when they got to Dante's name, Palmer mentioned a problem.

What a knucklehead was Brent's initial thought when he heard what Dante had done.

It was a thought he had often in this job of dealing with what basically were college kids. He had two doors to his office. One was usually open. That was known as the good door. The other door was for knuckleheads. The bad door. The knuckleheads would come to that door, knock on it three times, not two, not four, not too hard, not too softly, and wait for the fearsome Colonel Cummings to yell, "Report." Then they would enter Brent's office and stand at attention at the end of a long conference table, some already sweating at that point, some on the verge of tears.

"Report!" Brent hollered one day as a cadet waited outside.

"She's terrified, sir," one of Brent's staff members told him.

"Yes, she is," another staffer told him.

"Okay," Brent said, and in came a twenty-one-year-old woman whose contract was in jeopardy because she had given alcohol to an underage cadet.

"Why are you here?" Brent began.

"Alcohol violation, sir," she said, shaking as Brent paged through her file.

"You knew she was underage?"

"Yes, sir," she said.

She stood at parade rest, feet ten inches apart, legs straight but not locked, hands behind her.

"I knew the consequences. I was stupid. I made the decision," she said. "What I did was a mistake, and I own up to it."

"So what would you do?" Brent asked her. "I'm talking about selfless service, duty, honor, values. What would you do if you were in my position, representing the federal government?"

"I won't make this mistake again, sir," she said, and Brent said he would let her know of his decision, dismissed her, and asked for the underage cadet to be brought in.

"This might be interesting," a staffer said. "She deals with stress by laughing."

"She's definitely not taking this seriously," another said.

"Report!" Brent hollered, and in through the bad door came a young woman who said she drank because she had a lot going on in her life, and she got caught only because the empty bottles were clinking against each other when she took them to the trash.

"Do you understand how serious this is?" Brent asked.

"Yes, sir," she said.

"Do you?" Brent asked.

"Yes, sir," she repeated, and as she left his office a few minutes later, Brent saw her rolling her eyes.

"Whatever, old man," he said, laughing, after the bad door had closed.

It wasn't that Brent had become too old to understand what it was like to be twenty-one or twenty or even nineteen. When he was a student at a military college in Vermont, he played rugby, and hazing for new teammates one year involved them running around a field after a snowfall—shirtless, pantsless, holding a full cup of beer, and being pelted with snowballs. Brent's job was to check how much beer was in the cup at the end of the run, and if too much had spilled, that person would have to start over. "I won't make it if I have to do it again," Brent remembered one of the runners telling him as he held out his cup, which was empty. He was shivering and covered in red marks from being hit with snowballs.

"But there's no *beer*," Brent said, looking at the cup.

So he understood that young people do stupid things and make mistakes and then go on, as he had, to become colonels hollering the word "report."

"Report!"

In came a cadet in danger of losing his scholarship because he had been gaining weight, not working out, and rarely coming out of his dorm room.

"I messed up last semester," he said in a voice so quiet and lacking in emotion that Brent could barely hear him.

"I know you messed up. I got it. But what's going on?" Brent said. "Did you sleep last night? You look sleepy."

"That's just the way I look, sir," he said. "I have dark circles under my eyes."

"I'm worried. You don't look like you're with it right now," Brent said, and after a few minutes more, Brent grew so worried that he told his staff to make sure the cadet got in to see a counselor that afternoon.

"Report."

In came another cadet in danger of losing his scholarship over bad grades, and when Brent asked him to call home to discuss this with his parents, the cadet shrugged.

"Are you close to your parents?" Brent asked.

"No, sir, I'm not."

"Who do you look up to?" Brent asked. "Who's your mentor?"

"I don't have one, sir," he said, and Brent thought, *Could that be true? No one?*

"Report."

In came a cadet who said that he did have a mentor, his father, although his father had recently called him "a fucking dumbass."

And Brent was suddenly so glad his father had never called him such a thing.

"Report!"

In came four cadets who were facing suspensions for hazing.

"Don't smile. I'm pissed," Brent said and sent them back out the bad door. "That'll make them nervous," he said, waiting a minute before calling them back in one at a time.

"It was a team-building exercise," said the first. "That's how we looked at it."

Out he went.

"Fucking bullshit," Brent said.

In came the second.

"Sir, it was part of one of the traditions we do," he said, and went on to say there had been a scavenger hunt in the woods in which recruits had to find a family of Sasquatches. "I was one of the Sasquatches," he said.

"You mean Bigfoot?" Brent said, confused, trying to remember what a Sasquatch was.

"Yes, sir."

"And you're in an outfit?" he said, his confusion now about what they were wearing, wondering if the cadet had dressed up in some kind of furry getup.

"No, sir."

"Are you nude?"

"Yes, sir."

"So a grown man is naked? In the woods?"

"Yes, sir."

"Do you think that's weird?" Brent asked, and when the cadet didn't answer he tried again.

"Do you wear shoes?"

"Yes, sir."

Out he went.

"And the plot thickens," Brent said.

In came the next.

"Was there alcohol involved?" Brent asked.

"Not that I'm aware of, sir."

"Was there alcohol involved?" Brent repeated.

"I believe so, sir."

"Let me try again," Brent said and reminded the cadet of the honor code. "Was there alcohol involved?"

"Yes, sir," the cadet said.

And on it went.

One other thing Brent understood about being nineteen was the part these cadets couldn't understand, not yet, and, Brent hoped, not ever, the part about being in a war at the far end of an order that started with a president and worked its way down to generals, to colonels, to lieutenant colonels, to majors, to captains, to lieutenants, to sergeants, to corporals, and finally to a nineteen-year-old such as Duncan Crookston. He had been one of Brent's soldiers, and when the Humvee he was in exploded from an insurgent's bomb, he lost his right leg, his left leg, his right arm, and his lower left arm, and he was burned over most of what was left of his body. He didn't die, not then. It took thirty surgeries to keep him alive and almost five painful months for him to die, and after he did die, a memorial service was held back in Iraq, where Brent remembered picking up a general who'd flown in by helicopter to the lousy base where they'd been fighting for their lives.

"This is an infantry unit, right?" the general had asked him as they drove from the landing pad to the chapel.

"Yes, sir," Brent had said.

"There's not going to be crying, is there?" the general had asked. "I'm so sick of going to these things and seeing a bunch of boo-hooing. You're not a bunch of pussies, right?"

"Sir, I think you will see some tears," Brent had said and started to explain all that Duncan had meant and how brave his five-month fight to stay alive had been, but the general wasn't listening and Brent gave up. He had

despised that general, and he'd promised himself that
whoever he finally grew up to be after he'd recovered
from the war, he would never be a man such as that man.

"Report!"

Once again, the bad door opened, and in came Dante
Harris.

"OKAY, DON'T BEAT around the bush, don't bullshit
him, speak confidently but not cocky. All right? Because
otherwise, he'll tear you up," one of Brent's staffers had
told Dante just before he knocked. "Now to report, let's
roll through it," he'd continued, explaining about the
three knocks, not four, not two. "You're going to open
the door, you're going to walk through, you're going to
come to position, attention, salute, 'Sir, Cadet Harris reporting as ordered,' he's going to drop his salute, you
drop yours, he's probably going to say, 'Go to parade
rest.' All right? And then just take all commands from the
tower. All right? Good?"

"Good," Dante said.

By then, Brent knew all about Dante's case.

He knew that Dante had been arrested on one charge
of privacy invasion by unlawful eavesdropping or surveillance, which was a felony, and a second charge of trans-
mitting a photograph depicting nudity, a misdemeanor.
He knew Dante was facing up to six years in prison if he
didn't complete a pretrial diversion program and that he
had been suspended for two semesters by the university
for taking the photograph after being investigated on a
charge of sexual exploitation.

He knew that Richard Neikirk had written to school officials saying "I am not a vindictive person" and "my feelings are many, but just to mention a few—anger, disgust, disappointment, hurt, humiliation and disrespect."

Brent also knew that Dante had grown up poor in the particular kind of Southern poverty he'd been seeing since he was a child in Mississippi, that in spite of such circumstances Dante had earned a full scholarship because of his grades, that his scholarship was now in jeopardy, that he'd had an unblemished record right up to the moment he took the photograph, and that he had written two letters of apology to Neikirk, neither of which had been accepted.

And one other thing Brent knew, not from documents but from being a grown man, was how to urinate in a public building.

Until he saw the photograph, he imagined what Dante had done as something degenerate. After he saw it, it just seemed juvenile, and when he talked to a school lawyer about it, he asked the lawyer to imagine walking into a public restroom and seeing what Dante had seen. "I know what I would have done at that age," he said to the lawyer. "I would have run out and grabbed my buddy and been like, 'You gotta get in there, go go go go *go*, you gotta go in there, you gotta see.' That's what I would have done. 'Hey man, you gotta get in there, you're not gonna believe this, it's the funniest thing ever.' That's what I would have done. Not appropriate, immature, but that would have been my response when I was a twenty-year-old like Harris."

So what do you want to do about this, the lawyer had

asked, and Brent had said he wanted to ask Neikirk: Why weren't you in a stall with the door closed if you needed to lower your pants?

Mostly, he told the lawyer, he wanted to say: "You're ruining this fucking kid's life."

But instead he hollered, "Report!" and in through the bad door came Dante to the far end of the conference table, standing at attention and rendering a salute.

"Sir. Cadet Harris, reporting in, as ordered."

"Okay, Cadet Harris. Stand at parade rest," Brent said. "I understand you wanted to see me?"

"Yes, sir," Dante said.

"Okay, what do you want to see me about?"

"I was wondering if contracting was still possible with my circumstances."

"What are your circumstances?" Brent said. "You've never talked to me about the incident. So explain this incident to me."

"Um, I took a picture of Major Neikirk, and I showed it to three people, sent it to three people, and it got around school."

"What type of photo was it?" Brent asked.

"He was urinating at the latrine, sir," Dante said.

"At the urinal or in the stall?"

"The urinal."

"So why would you take a picture of it?"

"I just thought it was funny, sir."

"What was funny about it?"

"I just thought it was funny, sir. He was urinating with his pants below his waist."

"Okay. So what was your intent when you took it?"

Brent said, and when he saw the blank look on Dante's face, he said, "Dante, I'm trying to help you here. But you have got to be spot-on honest and talk to me like you need some help. You get me?"

"Yes, sir."

"Come sit down. Come over here. Right over here. Right here," Brent said, motioning to an empty chair at the conference table. "I want to understand your thoughts about why you did this. Talk to me. Tell me what's going on. I'm the only thing that may be able to give you some help, but I want to hear it from your words. So explain yourself, and talk to me."

"Yes, sir," Dante said. "Um, um, I just took a picture because I thought it was funny. I didn't expect it to get around the whole campus the way it did. It was just childish behavior on my part, sir. And then when it escalated, I came out and told them it was me, and stuff like that, I took the consequences that went with it."

"It's some pretty big consequences," Brent said.

"Yes, sir."

"Have you apologized to Major Neikirk?"

"I can't talk to him physically, but I've written him multiple apology letters," Dante said.

"I know all the details of this case, Dante," Brent said. "I know everything about it. I have seen it, it's been shared with me, I've seen the photo you've taken, I know everything about it. What I have to determine is what do we do, if anything, for you."

"Yes, sir."

"What have you learned from all this? Tell me. What have you learned?"

"Um, I've learned the consequences of the choices that you make, and how they affect you later in life. Like, I had a plan, and it all went away with just one choice. So I'm just learning to make better decisions. That's basically it, sir."

"Are you sorry for what happened?"

"Yes, sir. Deeply."

"Dante, look, there is an opportunity for you to contract," Brent said. "Okay? So that answers your question. But I'm not going to give it to you. You have to come earn it."

"Yes, sir."

"You get that?"

"Yes, sir."

"And to earn it, you've got to work your butt off. You have to work harder than everybody else. I'm just telling you. It's not going to be fair. Okay? But that's because of this event that's happened. All right? So you've got to overcome that and show me why we should offer you this contract."

"Yes, sir."

"Tell us why we should bother. That's on you," Brent said. "There's some pieces of this that I'm concerned about. I don't know if everything has been done the way I would want it to be done. But it ultimately comes back to the actions that you took when you took that photograph." He paused for a moment. "What was—again— the intent of that photograph?"

"I just thought it was funny, sir," Dante said.

"But what were you going to *do* with it?" Brent asked. "What was the *intent*?"

Dante was silent.

"You came out of the stall, right?"

"Yes, sir."

"You saw him doing something that looked strange, right?"

"Yes, sir."

"And he was compromised."

"Yes, sir."

"And you snapped the picture to do what with?"

"I just snapped the picture, and then I showed it to people, and that was it."

"But what was the *purpose* of showing the picture, Dante?"

"A reaction, sir, I guess," Dante said. He searched for an answer he hadn't given a dozen times already to the police who arrested him, the lawyer who took on his case, the university officials who had questioned him, or Neikirk in his letters of apology. "I guess it was just to belittle him."

"Okay. Right," Brent said. "Why?"

"I don't know," Dante said, beginning to tear up.

"All right," Brent said.

"It was just a moment, sir," Dante said.

"So what are you going to do?"

"Be a leader," Dante said.

"Yes. That's the most important thing," Brent said. "What I'm trying to do is get back before this event happened. Okay? I want to see that person that we saw before this happened, all right? And I want you to take the emotions that you have right there and channel them and use them to motivate yourself. Okay? Every morning, look at yourself in the mirror and say 'This sucks. I wish I had not done what I did. But I'm going to get myself so freaking squared away and I'm going to go out there and I'm going to show everybody that I am Dante Harris and I can do this.' "

Dante looked at him.

"That's what I want to see," Brent said. "All right, Dante?"

"Yes, sir."

"You got any questions?"

"No, sir."

"All right. Go back up to the end of the table and I'll dismiss you."

"Yes, sir."

"You're dismissed. Make it happen."

"Truth and wisdom, sir," Dante said, repeating the cadet motto, and out he went through the bad door.

"Well, that's that," Brent said.

But it wasn't.

More and more as the weeks went by, Brent found himself wondering: *What if Dante were white?*

"What if his name was Daniel Harris?" he began asking people as a way to get them to consider the question.

Would Daniel Harris have been forgiven more easily? Would Daniel Harris have been arrested? Would Daniel Harris be facing a threat of six years in prison? Would Daniel Harris have gotten the messages Brent knew Dante was getting after an article about his case appeared in the local paper? There were a lot of messages, they were venomous, and Dante had deleted all of them except for one, which had come from a woman so confident in what she had to say that she'd seen no need to mask her name or her vulgarities. "You stupid fucking n-----. Take your ass to brown or spelman," she had written, not bothering to hyphenate any of it, and every so often Dante would re-read what this complete stranger had felt compelled to say to him, even though it crushed him every time he did.

Crushed, though, wasn't the same as surprised, because if there was one fundamental difference between Dante and Brent, it was that Brent had been primed for success in his life and had suffered from his failures and that Dante had been primed for failure and suffered from his successes.

At some level, Brent understood that. For Dante, racism was a given, while for Brent it existed toward the edges of what he knew to be a privileged life. He couldn't help that. His skin color was his skin color. His upbringing was his upbringing. But neither of those had denied him a sense of empathy, and he continued to worry about Dante, even as he found himself embroiled in a second controversy at the school, also with racial overtones and, as causes go, probably just as lost.

IT INVOLVED AN insignia being used by a school club called the Blue Ridge Rifles. The club was a precision drill team made up of cadets who marched in parades with polished rifles that they spun and threw in the air, and their insignia, which always accompanied them, consisted of a red square with a blue diagonal slash across it and seven white stars running the length of the slash. "Holy cow. Really?" Brent thought the first time he saw it.

Here was the Confederate flag, if not exactly, then similar enough. He had grown up with that flag in Mississippi and had seen it proliferate since, not as a symbol of historic legacy but of modern hatred, and he wanted the insignia changed.

Others did not, including pretty much anyone he talked to at the university.

"This is just political correctness," one administrator told Brent about Brent's objection.

Another asked: Will every monument to the South have to be removed? Will it no longer be okay to sing "Dixie"? "My concern is, where does it stop?"

"I understand," Brent said, "but I am talking about an image of a flag that was used to counter the civil rights movement."

Another administrator, who said he was emboldened by Donald Trump's election, told Brent "We won," and pointed out that professors of military science like Brent move on to another assignment after a few years, whereas people employed by the university remain. "We'll just wait you out," he said.

Brent, though, had his own reason to be emboldened, a depressing conversation he'd had with his closest assistant, a black man named Kerry Dyer, whom Brent regarded as the finest soldier he'd ever worked with. They were driving through north Georgia, a landscape of pine forests and Trump signs, and Kerry told Brent about seeing the Blue Ridge Rifles insignia for the first time on his very first day of work. "Baby, do you see what I see?" his wife had asked him as they pulled in to a parking lot by the ROTC building.

And then Kerry had seen it too.

"Do I find the imagery offensive? Point blank yes," Kerry said to Brent.

Soon after that, Brent told Kerry of a plan he'd come up with to get rid of the insignia once and for all. All of the ROTC cadets were about to be issued new uniforms, courtesy of the Army that was spending $468,000 for them, and according to Army regulations, nothing could be part of those uniforms that wasn't Army-approved. That regulation was Brent's opening, and it didn't matter to him that no one had enforced the regulation before. He was going to. Once the new uniforms were distributed, the insignia wouldn't be allowed.

"Don't do it, sir. You're going to get too much heat for it. They're not going to understand," Kerry said, and the discouraged way he said it made Brent that much more determined.

So he went ahead, and when it became clear how upset the cadets were, he tried to explain his thinking to them during an assembly. "I'm born and raised in the state of Mississippi. I'm a son of the South. I have ancestors who fought for the Confederacy," he said, and paused for that to sink in. "And I'm very proud, grateful, that our Union held firm, that I stand here wearing the *Army* uniform."

One thing about Brent, he could make an inspirational speech like nobody else. "Suck it in!" he would often exhort the cadet corps at assemblies, and the room would be filled with the sound of seven hundred fifty cadets taking the deepest breath they could. "Let it out!" he would say after a moment, and the room would be filled with exhales and war cries.

But this time, there was too much collateral damage. If the Blue Ridge Rifles insignia had to be removed from uniforms, so, all of a sudden, did the insignias of the nine other cadet organizations, such as the honor society, and what had the honor society ever done to offend anyone?

"He killed fifty years of tradition," Tom Palmer, the commandant, said one day. "Is the problem over? No." And then, referring to the pressures he was under, added: "The alumni haven't weighed in yet. Let's see what the alumni do."

The alumni: "A fat fuck who doesn't donate any money and says, 'We didn't march like that when *I* was there,'" was what Brent had to say about some of those alumni, but soon Palmer was announcing the new uniform guidelines he had come up with, without Brent's input. On Mondays, Tuesdays, and Wednesdays, when cadets were required to wear their Army-supplied uniform, the insignia wouldn't be allowed. On Thursdays and Fridays, when cadets wore school-issued uniforms, they could wear whatever they wanted. And weekends, too.

The insignia also remained on the flag the cadets carried whenever they performed. And on a wall outside the building where they stored their equipment, and on stickers they smoothed onto laptops, coffee mugs, water bottles, and whatever else a cadet wanted to attach a sticker to. "It's a smaller victory than I want it to be," Brent said, and so it wasn't settled at all, and he carried his soreness about that everywhere, including home, including to bed, where one night, here came another dream. He'd been having his dream, the bad one, more and more. The blackness. The sound of being laughed at.

———

"REPORT," BRENT SAID, and in came a cadet named
Jesse Briggs who was the leader of the Blue Ridge Rifles,
and who was dead-set against changing the insignia, but
that wasn't why Brent wanted to see him.

"I need to know every single detail," Brent said, and
the cadet, who didn't seem scared in the least to be called
in by his commander, started going through it. A girl. A
fight. Drinking, driving, speeding, losing control, ending
up in the trees. A cop with a breathalyzer machine and
being charged with DUI.

"So you were pretty liquored up," Brent said, and if he
was at all sympathetic, it was because he, too, had once
been in a fight with a girl after a few beers when he was
twenty-one, and at the wheel of a speeding pickup truck
that went off the road. In his case, his truck rolled over a
few times, he was banged up, the girl was bloodied from
a cut on her forehead, and they walked in a daze until
they found a cabin where two couples were inside playing
cards. "I had a flat tire," he told them, and that was the
end of it. No police. No charges. No girlfriend, either,
not after that, which brought him to the life he'd had
with Laura, with Emily, with Meredith, and now with
Jesse Briggs.

They were alike in so many ways—same height, same
weight, same occasional cockiness—but so much had
changed between his accident and Jesse's. For one thing,
drunk driving was treated much more seriously. For another, the cops who didn't show up at Brent's accident
did show up at Jesse's. And a third difference: The cops

who always came now often came with cameras rolling. Sometimes those cameras recorded cops doing the worst things imaginable, which had led to many of the protests against police brutality and police racism growing across the country, and sometimes they showed cops at their best, which was the case of the Georgia state trooper who had approached Jesse, still dazed, in his ruined car.

"Mr. Briggs?"

"Yes, sir."

"You all right?"

"Yes, sir."

"What happened, man?"

That was the beginning of the audio. The video, taken from a dashboard camera, showed a raw rainy day, a rural two-lane road, and way to the left, a Dodge Challenger in the treeline.

"Okay," the trooper said. "How much alcohol you had to drink?"

"None, sir."

"None?"

"About one beer, maybe. I had like twelve ounces."

"Okay. All right. You blow an Alco-Sensor for me?"

Pause.

"Yes, sir," Jesse said.

"Blow," the trooper said. "Blow harder. Blow blow blow blow blow blow blow blow blow blow. Good job. What's that say?"

"One point four eight?" Jesse said, reading the number.

"One point four eight," the trooper said, aware that the legal limit was point zero eight. "And you said one beer?"

"Yes, sir."

"How long ago was that one beer?"

"Probably thirty minutes."

"All right, man, come on over here. Come on, Mr. Briggs. We're gonna go right down in front of my patrol car."

"Yes, sir."

"Will you do a field sobriety test for me?"

"Yes, sir."

"You're gonna walk this line right here," the trooper said. "Now when I tell you to begin, I want you to take nine heel-to-toe steps out this line. Okay?"

"Yes, sir."

"I want you to count your steps out loud."

"Yes, sir," Jesse said.

"One. Two. Three. Until you get to nine," the trooper said. "Begin when you're ready."

"One," Jesse said, taking his first step. "Nine," he said as he got to nine, and kept going. "Eleven steps," the trooper said, watching, counting. "Twelve steps. Thirteen steps. Fourteen. Fifteen. Sixteen. Seventeen. Eighteen. Nineteen."

Finally, Jesse stopped.

"Twenty steps," the trooper said.

"All right, turn around for me, please," the trooper said, handcuffing Jesse, and now Jesse was saying to Brent, "I was very respectful the entire process. I knew I was in the wrong." He explained he had completed a DUI course, had done community service, was waiting to go to trial, and was hoping the charge would be reduced to reckless driving, which would allow him to continue as a cadet.

"What outcome do you want?" Brent asked.

"To commission as an officer," Jesse said, and Brent said to him a version of what he had said to Dante.

"We all see potential in you. What I want you to do is show us your desire," he said. "It's a burden, but it's a burden you placed on yourself."

"Yes, sir," he said, and away he went to prove his desire, beginning with Blue Ridge Rifles practice.

They were out on the drill field in the center of campus, their flag waving in sight of the other seven thousand students on campus who weren't in ROTC. They were spinning twelve-pound rifles like batons, and all of them had nicknames they'd been given on their T-shirts.

Texaco was one of those names. "I don't even have to explain it because it's so apparent," the cadet who was called that said, and then explained it. He was of Indian descent, and Indian people often worked at 7-Elevens, and 7-Elevens often sold Texaco gasoline. "Obviously," he said.

Capo was another, so named because that cadet supervised some of the other cadets, and "kapo" was a term for certain Jews in concentration camps who were put in charge of other Jews. Like the others, his shirt also had a number on it, and his number was 999, in reference to a movie scene in which Hitler yelled "Nein nein nein."

So they weren't the most sensitive group. "Childish" and "stupid" Brent had concluded about what Dante had done, and the conclusion about the Blue Ridge Rifles by a cadet whose given nickname was Magilla Gorilla and who insisted the name had nothing to do with his being black, that it was because he and the cartoon character shared a fondness for bow ties, was similar. "Some might say we're the misfits of the corps," he said.

The misfits, then. Every one of them took great joy in what they did, and if they had anything in common beyond their skill at spinning rifles, it was their devotion to an insignia that had been designed in the 1950s, when Georgia was still legally segregated, in honor of some long-dead volunteers from the area who called themselves the Blue Ridge Rifles and in 1861 had marched off with their rifles to join the Confederate Army.

In other words, Jesse said, it was an insignia that honored history. "This isn't a Confederate flag, plain and simple," he said. He felt strongly about that and wasn't ready to give up on it, and when it came time for the first public performance of the year, their insignia was still on the flag as Tom Palmer announced, "Ladies and gentlemen, the Blue Ridge Rifles."

Hundreds of people applauded, and Brent watched them march in, and, next to him, Kerry Dyer watched too.

"YES! YES! Victory is ours!!!" Kerry had texted Brent a few days before, in a brief moment of optimism about the plan Brent had come up with to get the insignias stripped off the uniforms. "All I can say and what so many other Cadets and Soldiers can say silently is THANK YOU."

"AM I THE ONE who's wrong? Am I the one who's missing something?" Brent asked one day. It wasn't an exercise in self-abasement, just genuine curiosity. He was in his truck on his way to Fort Benning in western Georgia, trying to figure out why a road he had driven on so many times over the years felt different. The sky was still that Georgia blue, but the blue felt more electric. The pine trees were bending as usual in the breeze, but they felt shakier somehow, less rooted, and it wasn't only because of the Trump signs still nailed to their trunks or planted at their bases, it was everything.

Eleven years before, when he left in early 2007 to fight in the Iraq War, the country whose values he was defending felt different. "It felt"—he searched around for a few seconds—"clean. No, that's not the right word." He kept searching and at last settled on a way to describe what the country felt like now.

"It's slipping," he said.

It was, or he was, or something was, on this day in March 2018. "I'm surprised at how many people I know, love, trust, admire who are not using critical thinking to say *Wait a minute*," he said, because, really, how at this point in American history could anyone think that the Blue Ridge Rifles insignia was a good idea?

And how could there be so many who did?

"The symbol has become a weapon," he said of the Confederate flag.

He was nearing the city of Columbus. More Trump signs. So many of them, still, as if the election were a few weeks in the future rather than sixteen months in the past. "Chaos leadership" was what Brent called the Trump presidency so far, and he was starting to wonder if the leader Trump would fully become would be a version of the general who had asked Brent if his grieving soldiers were a bunch of pussies. Maybe Trump would. Probably so. Probably Trump had always been that general. By that point, Trump had already uttered his "very fine people" line about some of the white nationalists and neo-Nazis who had marched in Charlottesville, Virginia. But maybe Trump would surprise him as another general had, one gruff in reputation and intimidating in person who was visiting the university and asked Brent about the insignia. "What's going on with the Blue Ridge Rifles crap?" was how the general phrased his question, and after Brent had filled him in, he'd said, "Fuck 'em. You're doing the right thing."

So you never knew.

"It's too soon to know," Brent said.

Deep down, though, he pretty much knew.

At a gas station now, he checked his messages and saw one listing the names of cadets who had missed physical training that morning. One of them was Dante.

Brent was surprised. Just the other morning he had joined Dante's platoon at sunrise training to check up on him, and for an hour they'd gone hard at it. Running the bleachers. Lifting weights. Push-ups. Sit-ups. Jumping rope. Throwing a medicine ball. Finally came a game of dodgeball with partly deflated rubber balls that made them easier to grab and more stinging when they hit, and here came Dante at full speed, thinner than he'd been, fitter than he'd been, ball in hand, looking for a target, finding one, locking in, arm back, throwing an absolute missile, and all of a sudden everyone was saying, "Whoa! Whoa!" because the target was Brent and if he hadn't raised his arm at the last moment that missile would have smacked him square in the face. "Oh my God," Dante had said when he realized who he'd taken aim at, but Brent had laughed it off and walked away thinking Dante was really getting squared away.

But now this. Physical training wasn't an option. It was mandatory.

"What the fuck, dude?" Brent said.

Had Dante forgotten what Brent had said to him? Had he forgotten what he had promised?

"Not good," Brent said, staring at the message. He looked up and noticed two people getting into the car next to his, a bright blue Mustang convertible. Its top was down, the sun was making everything shiny, the driver was maybe in his early twenties, the woman he was with was the same, and they were both beautiful and laughing and looking at each other in a way that made Brent quickly look away. *Is there a better age to be?* he thought, looking back down at his phone, and meanwhile, a few miles from there, in a different part of Columbus, was a small brick house where Dante had grown up, and where he'd returned to one night, unlocked the front door, and had it pushed back in his face.

He was at that moment a senior in high school who was living in a different kind of chaos than whatever chaos Brent was feeling—a crowded house, three siblings by different absentee fathers, little money, drugs, alcohol, police visits, protective services visits, and at the center of it all, a mother who was sitting wordlessly on a couch as her son, her point of pride with his A average at the most competitive high school in Columbus, tried to push his way inside. On the other side of the door was his mother's latest boyfriend inexplicably pushing back, and when Dante finally overpowered him and got in, the boyfriend told him to get his stuff and leave. There was no explanation. Just: leave. His mother was still saying nothing, not a word, still on the couch, not getting up, so after Dante looked at her for help, and it registered she would not be fighting for him, he found some trash bags, filled them with his clothing, walked out, reached the street, and made a right.

"Fuck," Brent said again, wondering if he had been too generous toward Dante, if Dante had been playing him—and somewhere a few miles away was the place Dante walked to after leaving his house, a playground with a sliding board that had a covering over it, like a tube, which was where he began sleeping, alone, and telling no one what had happened because there was no one to tell.

"I'm not going to contract the guy," Brent said—and somewhere was the road Dante had been walking down after school on his way back to the playground for his third night when the mother of another student passed by, recognized him, and asked if he needed a ride home. And then after dropping him off at his house, she happened to watch in her mirror as he veered away and began walking in a different direction. And then she circled back to him and asked if he was okay, and when he said he was, asked him again, and then, when he told her no, no he wasn't, took him to her home, gave him a room to sleep in, gave him a safe place to live until he graduated from high school, suggested one day that maybe the military would be a good option for him, and helped him write the essay that along with his nearly perfect grades got him a full scholarship to college.

It was the first true act of kindness Dante had experienced in his life.

Now came another.

"I don't know. I'll give him the benefit of the doubt," Brent said, and once again, Dante was safe.

THAT NIGHT, THE DREAM came again. The worst one. The black was especially black. The laughter was especially mocking. All of it was so frightening it made Brent run from bed, but once he was fully awake, he did what he always did: took deep breaths, tried to push it from his mind, and moved on to whatever was next.

His time at the university was almost over. That administrator had been right—professors of military science don't last forever. He would be moving on to another assignment, this time in Jerusalem, his last in the Army before retiring and becoming a civilian, and in his final days at the university, he was down to paperwork and ceremonies.

One involved the ceremony for officially contracting cadets. "Are you ready?" Brent asked forty of them as their families looked on. "Are you ready to serve?" "Yes, sir," they hollered, and there would have been forty-one except that Dante wasn't among them because he still hadn't gotten final approval. Something about there being missing signatures, and he still hadn't completed his pre-trial diversion program. Dante didn't fully understand,

but it didn't matter. It's not like he had anyone coming to
the ceremony to watch, and he was otherwise set. His
grades for the semester were all A's, and a few days before, he'd passed his physical fitness test. "Everything's
looking good," Dante said with the patience of someone
who knew patience.

Meanwhile, with the impatience of someone who knew
the Army, Brent wondered where the paperwork was.

A week or so left now in the semester, and it was time
for the final performance of the year by Jesse Briggs, Texaco, Capo, Magilla Gorilla, and the rest of the Blue Ridge
Rifles. Quietly, some of the cadets had taken it upon
themselves to redesign the insignia, in case it came to
that. "The era we're in," Jesse called it dismissively. "It
makes me very bitter." But for now the old insignia was
still in place as the announcer, who this time happened to
be Richard Neikirk, said, "Ladies and gentlemen, the
Blue Ridge Rifles," and Brent watched that flag with his
own version of bitterness, hoping it was the last time
anyone would see it.

One day left now before he was through.

"Any update on CDT Harris for contracting?" Brent
wrote in an email to an Army lawyer who had gotten involved in Dante's case. "I'm mission complete here at
UNG tomorrow." He waited for a reply, but after a few
minutes he had to go. The foyer of the ROTC building
was packed with cadets and their families. This was commissioning day, when graduating cadets were sworn one
by one into the Army, and Brent had dozens of ceremonies to oversee. "Congratulations," he said to one of
those cadets, who a few months before had been one of

those in the woods searching for Sasquatch. "You haven't found any creatures, have you?"

He ducked back into his office.

There was no reply from the lawyer, so he called.

No answer.

Back out to the foyer.

All day long, Brent kept checking, but there was no word and not much he could do. He'd been pressing Dante's case for months now, and it was finally dawning on him what the problem was, something maddeningly technical involving a waiver that needed to come from the commanding general in charge of all ROTC cadets, not just at Brent's school but across the nation. There were thousands of cadets, and thousands of problems, and for whatever reason the problem of Dante Harris hadn't gotten the general's attention.

Back out to the foyer for another commissioning, where Brent noticed Jesse Briggs walking around.

Back into his office.

"Let's get Mr. Briggs in," he told his staff. "Have him come in the bad door."

Three knocks.

"Report!"

In came Jesse, wondering what he had done.

"Grab a seat," Brent said.

"Yes, sir."

"All right, look. First of all, where were you the other day when you were supposed to meet with me?"

"I went back to my room after studying and then had fallen asleep to take a nap and slept through my alarm, sir."

"All right, that was a bad time for you to be asleep. Pissed me the freak off. I was bringing you down here to give you a piece of what I think is some decent news over-all," Brent said and then noticed Jesse's arm. "Why do you have a bandage on?"

"I was playing in the woods, sir."

"You were playing in the woods?"

"I was going on an adventure. Climbing some rock walls. And I scratched my arm."

"How bad's the injury?"

"It's not bad, sir."

"You're a knucklehead," Brent said. "I can't tell you how angry I am at you for blowing me off the other day because I was sitting here on the phone with my boss, talking and pleading your case, because you crossed the one line you can't cross. DUI? That's it. But my argument has been, 'Hey he's young, he made a mistake, he owned the mistake, he's pushed hard, he soldiered on, let's give him a second opportunity.' And I convinced him. He said, 'Yeah, you got a good point.'"

That was the good news. As long as Jesse's case could be knocked down to reckless driving—and Jesse thought it would be, because at his most recent court hearing, even the prosecutor was moved to remark after seeing the dashcam video, "He was very polite . . . very respect-ful . . ."—he could continue toward the outcome of be-coming a commissioned officer.

"Then," Brent continued, "you're supposed to come down and see me and you never show up because you fell asleep and you didn't wake up. The opportunities you're getting? I don't know why you're getting them. Okay?

You've got something that makes you very fortunate. So that irritated me. You could tell."

"Yes, sir," Jesse said.

"But here's the deal. Here's what I was going to tell you, and this is it," Brent said. "This is your shot. Okay? There is no other shot. You get me?"

"Yes, sir."

"You clear with me?"

"Yes, sir."

"All right. Good luck," Brent said, dismissing the knucklehead, and now, down to his final hours, he called the boss he had called about Jesse to make one last plea for Dante.

"I guess nothing back on old Harris?" he began, asking if there'd been any word from the commanding general. "Yeah . . . Yeah . . . Do you think they'll let him contract at all? . . . Right, right . . . He doesn't *have* family . . . He doesn't have advocates . . . He only has me and you . . . Yeah . . . If we don't give this kid this chance, he's done. This is his life chance. I don't want to be dramatic, but it is . . ."

He hung up.

"Fuck. I'm out of time. I don't know what else to do."

The foyer was filled with people. He needed to be out there, but he stayed at his desk. His office was packed up, ready for its next occupant, who Brent understood would see Dante as an inherited problem and nothing more.

"I'm going to break his heart when I tell him," he said.

"I don't know how to tell him."

"I guess I just say it."

But he put it off as long as he could, instead going out into the foyer to commission one of the cadets who had asked Dante to send her the photo. Dante was there too, among the people watching, and he applauded along with everyone else when she said to her parents, "You guys have supported me in my career with such understanding. I can't thank you enough."

"I love you, Mom," another cadet said as he was about to be commissioned, and Dante watched that one too.

School was done for the semester. Dante could have gone back to Columbus, but there was no reason to, so he kept hanging out and watching until he was told that Brent wanted to see him in his office.

He went in through the good door.

"Hey, Dante, come on in and grab a seat," Brent said, still unsure of how to say what he was about to say, and then he just said it. "I have not gotten permission yet to contract you. I thought I would have that approval before now. But it has not come."

He paused in case Dante wanted to say something. Sometimes Dante had the wearied look of someone used to pain. This time he had the look of someone bracing for it. But he didn't say anything, so Brent went on.

"I admire what you've done," he said. "I see great potential in you. I'm hopeful, I'm so very hopeful that you will be in the United States Army. But Dante, I'm not sure I'm going to be able to make that happen, and I'm about out of time."

Another pause.

"That's just where it is. It's where it sits right now. I wanted you to know that."

Still Dante said nothing, and Brent went on for a while more.

"I've told you before that what you did that got us to this point, that's behind us, but you've got to stay focused and leaning forward," he said.

"Whatever comes out of this, I want you to know that you have my support," he said.

"I think you have a bright future ahead of yourself, and I'd just tell you to stay positive and know that there are people out there that will see what I have seen in you," he said.

"Okay?" he said, and finally, Dante had something to say.

"Yes, sir," he said.

"You got any questions?"

"No, sir," Dante said.

"I'm proud of you," Brent said.

"Thank you, sir," Dante said, and while Brent stayed in his office, head down, clearing his throat, feeling defeated, Dante walked out the good door and into the crowded foyer. He wanted some privacy, and the bathroom was right there. That would have been the easy thing to do, duck inside, go past that urinal and into a stall, but the moment felt cruel enough already, so instead he went outside into a quiet courtyard behind the building. A family was out there, and he waited at the edge of the courtyard until they left. Then he broke down crying, unaware that another cadet was in the courtyard too.

It was Jesse Briggs.

He walked toward Dante. He had no idea of what had just happened, but that didn't stop him. Without asking anything, without saying anything, he wrapped his arms around Dante and pulled him close, and now Dante was overcome even more.

THE BEST DAY Brent had had in Iraq had begun with a phone call.

"Izzy?" he yelled into his phone over the sounds of another day in war. "Izzy?"

The call was from one of his unit's interpreters, an Iraqi national who had left the base for a few days to go see his family in Baghdad and whose apartment building had been blown up by a massive car bomb. Twenty-five people had been killed, the building was on fire, and Izzy was on a street corner with one of his daughters who was covered in blood because a piece of a window of that apartment building had gone into the left side of her head. Izzy had been in the midst of telling Brent the hospitals were filled and he didn't know what to do, that his daughter might be dying and he needed help, when the line went dead.

"Izzy," Brent said, calling him back, "bring your daughter here."

It was as audacious a thing as Brent had said during his entire time in Iraq. Technically, the girl wasn't allowed to set foot on an American base, but Brent began trying to find a way. He called doctors to ask if they would treat the girl. He tracked down the officer whose approval would be needed for someone not in the military to get through the gate without being detained or shot. No one seemed to know the right thing to do, but he did know. He kept making calls and pleading, and finally, at the end of that day, after he had run out the gate and past the blast walls to bring Izzy and his daughter to the aid station, after doctors had dug out a long piece of glass and said the girl would be okay and Izzy had bowed his head and wiped his eyes and said to Brent, "Thank you, sir," Brent had said quietly, "Man, I haven't felt this good since I got to this hellhole."

Now, a week after he had sent Dante away, came the best day Brent would have as professor of military science. Somehow, Brent's boss had taken what Brent had said to heart and managed to see the commanding general. Somehow the commanding general had been persuaded by what he heard and said yes to a waiver, and now Dante and Brent were back in Brent's office, and Brent was saying, "Well, this is a good day for you."

How did good days happen, both in hellholes and out of them? On this day, here was how:

"I just signed your contracting paperwork, so technically we're done. But I'm going to do a little ceremony," Brent said. "Ready?"

"Yes, sir," Dante said.

"You sure?"

"Yes, sir," Dante said.

"Come to position at attention and raise your right hand and repeat after me," Brent said, launching into the oath he believed in so fiercely, and a moment later the Army had its newest contracted cadet.

Brent understood there was no way to know what would happen next. Izzy had taught him that. The one benefit of being an interpreter, as Izzy had been, was that if you lasted at least a year and had the right recommendation letters, you would be considered one day for refugee status to the United States. That had been Izzy's illuminating hope. He had a storage locker on base, and mixed in with the things he'd bought from the shop on base to take to his daughter—lotion for her scars, hair ribbons, pencils—were nine such letters he'd collected from American soldiers, all of them glowing, one of which described how his "patriotism landed him in the hospital as he was beaten almost to death for trying to gather information about our area of operations." But he never got permission, he never got out of Iraq, and he eventually died there, in the company of his family and those worthless letters.

As for Dante:

"He came from trash, he is trash, he'll go back to trash," was one faculty member's prediction of what would happen once Brent was gone and Dante had no protectors.

It was as heartless a thing as Brent had ever heard, but now, as he clapped Dante on the back, and Dante smiled in a way he'd not seen him smile, he knew that at least in this moment, goodness had won out.

This was the world Brent had been promised, and on this day in May 2018—the very same day that a president who was maybe grunting and maybe in socks and boxer shorts tweeted "I now have my best Poll Numbers in a year"—it still felt as possible to him as ever.

CHAPTER 3

BRENT WAS DRIVING. Laura was next to him. Emily and Meredith were still young and buckled into their car seats. There was a shimmer in the road up ahead, which turned out to be water. "Don't drive through it," Laura said, but Brent kept going. *"Don't,"* she said again, realizing the water was a flood, but Brent was no longer in the car, and before she could figure out where he had gone, the car was filling with water and sinking. The girls were looking at her, and she understood. She was alone now. Everything was up to her. She reached toward the backseat. She knew she had time to save only one of them.

Who was it going to be?

So Laura had her dreams too, and when she woke up on this day, she really was alone and everything really was up to her. Brent was overseas, in Jerusalem, and in his absence, in case someone were to break in, she had been sleeping with a hammer under the mattress with its handle poking out so she could grab it, a folding knife of Brent's she sometimes stashed under his pillow and sometimes held in her hand, and a can of wasp killer on the nightstand that according to the label "Sprays up to 22 feet!"

"Meredith?" she called out.

No time to think about a dream. No time to think about anything other than the school bus that soon would be arriving. Get Meredith up. Pick out Meredith's clothing. Hold out Meredith's shirt for her and help her slip her arms in because of balance issues. Help her with her pants. Get her medication. Remind her when she's coming down the stairs to be careful on the steps. Make her a gluten-free breakfast and be sure to give her a choice. "Mer? Chicken or bacon?" Pack Meredith's lunch. Pack Meredith's backpack. Comb Meredith's hair. Brush Meredith's teeth with toothpaste that tastes like bubblegum and has a princess on the tube. That was Laura's life on this day, a day when Donald Trump would be tweeting "Today we celebrate the lives and achievements of Americans with Down Syndrome. @VP and I will always stand with these wonderful families, and together we will always stand for LIFE!"

Everything was about the bus.

Get Meredith on it.

And then be there waiting when it came back in the afternoon because to miss that bus, even by a minute, would mean she had made the choice she never made in her dream.

——

A FEW WEEKS BEFORE, Trump had tweeted something else. "Poll: Suburban women are coming back into the Republican Party in droves 'because of the Wall and Border Security. 70% support Border Security and the Wall,' " it said.

It was a tweet that in spite of its verified inaccuracies had been marked as "Favorite" 110,799 times and retweeted 24,312 times. More central to Laura's life, it was also a tweet that, whether it was about the morality of building a border wall, as Trump said, or fearmongering, as others said, its perfect target was Pleasantville.

Laura was the one who'd found the neighborhood while Brent was overseas finishing an assignment before starting at the University of North Georgia. It would be a forty-five-minute drive for him each way, but the special education programs in schools closer to his job seemed lacking to Laura, and the one Meredith would be attending was highly regarded. Plus, Atlanta was forty-five minutes in the other direction—close enough to go to concerts and plays, far enough to feel removed.

There were things Laura didn't know when she chose the house, including the shameful history of the county she'd be living in, beginning with the lynching in 1912 of a black man accused, with no evidence, of raping and beating a white woman, who ultimately died of her injuries. About twelve thousand people were living in the county then, a thousand of whom were black, and within a few weeks of the lynching of the man, who was hanged from a pole after being beaten with a crowbar and shot, nearly every black person had vanished from the county, not so much leaving as fleeing. There were house bombings, church burnings, and night raids carried out by mobs armed with guns, torches, and dynamite. There were more killings, too, including the hanging on public gallows, as several thousand people watched from the surrounding hills, of two teenagers said to also have been involved in the assault on the woman. So deep was the intimidation against black people, and so lasting was the terror it created, that no black person lived in the county again for the next seventy-five years. Only after a series of protests in 1987 did that begin to change, but so slowly as to be barely happening at all. By 1990, there were still only a dozen black people. By 2000, the number had grown, but only to 720, and then, at last, came the assimilation that had been happening in other parts of the South. By 2010, the number was above four thousand, and by the time Laura found the house in 2015, in a county that had grown to an overall population of over two hundred thousand, the black population was around seven thousand, the Hispanic population was nearly twenty thousand, the Asian population was above twenty-two thousand, and a county that had been 99.9 percent white in 1987 was now 75 percent white.

That was the county Laura had seen, the one it was becoming rather than the one it had been, and when she saw the house, and the trees surrounding it, and the front porch Brent wanted, and an office for the online teaching she did at a couple of colleges, and a backyard big enough for, say, a trampoline, it seemed as secluded and safe a place as she could have hoped for, with a kind of quiet that hadn't yet started to feel under threat.

It had those good schools, for both girls.

It had a park nearby with walking and running trails.

And it had that bus.

"Come on, Mer."

Right on time.

THERE WENT THE BUS, around the cul-de-sac and disappearing around the corner, which meant Laura had seven hours and fifty minutes until its return.

"Oh, crap," she said, in her car now, pulling up to the assisted living facility where her mother, Nancy Sargent, lived, and where two ambulances were at the entrance blocking it. "Dammit. Who are they hauling off?"

She didn't like sounding that way. But time was always so tight. The worst was when residents were sitting out front and every rocking chair was filled with friendly people who wanted to say hello, hello, hello, hello.

"I think you're just stressed. You have a lot on your plate. You need to find a way to reduce your stress," she remembered a doctor once telling her, and she knew the doctor meant well, but she couldn't help thinking that one way to reduce her stress would be to stop going to a doctor who kept repeating the word "stress."

Inside to the front desk to check in.

"Hi, Laura . . ."

That took a few minutes.

Past the fireplace area where Brent had given a talk one Veterans Day to residents who came in wheelchairs, on walkers, and with Life Alert pendants around their necks like dog tags, including a woman who had caught

Brent up short with her prayer: "We pray especially for the young men and women, in the thousands, who are coming home from Iraq with injured bodies and traumatized spirits. Bring solace to them, O Lord . . ."

Past the dining room, up the elevator, and past the room Laura called "the death room" because of how frequently it got new residents. Her mother's room was next door, furnished with a few things Brent had hauled back from her home in Kansas, where she had raised four daughters, was active in the League of Women Voters and a book club called the Wild Women's Literary Society, volunteered as a poll worker, did yoga. Now life was a sofa from that house, a recliner, a nightstand with a photograph of her dead husband, and a single bed.

"Oh, hi," she said when Laura walked in, sounding a little surprised even though she knew Laura was coming. She was eighty-eight years old, a little deaf, a little vacant in the eyes, memory fading, and a little confused when Laura asked her about some medical forms that needed to be filled out so Laura could make a doctor's appointment for her as soon as possible and take her to the doctor and sit with her at the doctor and take her back to the facility and get home before Meredith's bus arrived.

"Did you finish that paperwork?" Laura asked her.

"What?" her mother said pleasantly.

"Did you finish the paperwork?"

"Let me check."

A minute later:

"I think I found it but I didn't know what it was for. Do I need to check something there?"

"No," Laura said, looking at all of the blank spaces.

"Okay. Thank you. Do you want me to keep it, or you'll take it?"

"I have to figure out when you had your flu shot. And your pneumonia vaccine."

"Okay. I think I got it. But I don't know."

A few minutes after that:

"How are you doing otherwise?" Laura asked.

"Okay."

"Anything exciting today? Or just the usual?"

A few minutes later:

"All right, well, I don't have anything else," Laura said.

"I don't know if I do or not," her mother said.

Another few minutes:

"Okay. All right," Laura said. "Well . . ."

"That was a nice day yesterday," her mother said. "With the sun."

"It was nice," Laura said. "Did you go outside?"

"Oh, yes," her mother said.

Another few minutes:

"All right. Well I'm going to head out. I need to go run some more errands."

"Okay."

"Unless you need something."

"I don't need anything."

"All right. Let me know if you need anything."

"So, thank you for coming over."

Another few minutes, both of them in the elevator now, on the way down to the lobby. "Swedish meatballs yesterday?" Laura asked, looking at the week's menu posted on an elevator wall.

"I didn't have those. I had the chicken," her mother said, laughing, and a few minutes later Laura was outside, where a woman was being loaded into one of the ambulances.

"See, I just . . . I don't . . . I can't . . . ugh," she said, watching. "I don't ever want to be . . . Maybe when you get there, it's different."

Six and a half hours left now. Off to the pharmacy, the grocery store, here, there, this, that, and home to walk the puppy, a beagle named Sampson, that Brent had insisted they get when he'd come home from Jerusalem for Thanksgiving and had seen how down in the dumps Laura had seemed. "I think you need a friend," he'd said, and she'd thought, *Do I? Is that what I need?*

FOR YEARS THEY'D had another dog, a black Lab named Tucker, who had recently died. He was a sweet old dog who'd been wheezing more and more as his heart gave out, and when the vet was euthanizing him, Meredith was there too, petting him and crying ever so slightly. It was unusual for her. One effect of her version of Down syndrome was a pain response so delayed that at school one day, outside for recess, she had stood unaware on a nest of fire ants, which began biting their way up her legs. Only when she was covered in hundreds of bites had she indicated she was hurt. "Ow," she said. There were no tears, though, only that word. Once, after surgery, she did cry when nurses tried to help her sit up, telling her that she could go home when she was able to sit up. "You've got to let us know if it hurts, honey," Laura remembered saying to her, and at first Meredith did well, but at some point, as the nurses kept moving her, "you could see this tear in her eye and then rolling down her cheek, and I said, 'Meredith, does it hurt?' and she said, 'Yes,'" Laura said. "And it broke my heart because she's such a tough little girl."

A "Yes," a quiet "Ow," or nothing at all. That was what you got out of Meredith in her extreme moments, and yet for the first eight years of her life, she had been an absolute chatterbox, right up until she had a teaching aide in her classroom Laura had had a bad feeling about. Was there abuse? In all the years since, Laura suspected there was but had no way to know. What she did know was that the aide had been fired after a parent walked into the classroom one day and saw the aide shaking the chair Meredith was seated in. Laura happened to have arrived at the school as the aide was being escorted out. "I didn't do what they said I did," she said as she passed by Laura, and then Meredith stopped talking, and a speech therapist, a psychologist, and a psychiatrist all suggested she could be experiencing selective mutism, a condition brought on by anxiety or a traumatic event.

The mysteries of that girl. There were so many, hidden somewhere behind a face so trusting and without guile it sometimes made Laura physically ache. If in the years ahead Meredith could learn to read at the sixth grade level, and tell time, and figure out money, and get some type of job, that was what Laura wanted for her. As for talking, it wasn't as if she never talked, but her sentences were always short and whispered. Antianxiety medications hadn't helped. Neither had therapists, although Laura kept trying. Occupational therapy. Swim therapy. Horse riding therapy. It was just the way Meredith was and would be, but at least as she got older she had taken to texting on her iPad, which meant if Laura had to run out somewhere, she could send texts to Meredith to make sure she was all right.

"Well this is taking forever," she texted Meredith one day when there was no school, at yet another doctor's appointment with her mother. "Please text me if you need me and I will come right home."

"where tucker?" Meredith wrote back.

"Are you ok? Yes or no."

"yes where tucker"

"He lives in heaven with Jesus."

Another day, another appointment.

"Hey grandma's appointment is taking longer. I won't be home until about 11. Are you ok?"

"yes where tucker"

"His spirit is in heaven with Jesus and his body is in the box downstairs."

Another appointment. There were more and more of them now for her mother.

"I should be home around 12 and will fix you lunch."

"turkey and salami where tucker"

"Ok I have turkey and salami. Tucker lives in heaven. See you soon."

"mom sampson eating my turkey," Meredith texted another day when Laura was in the car with her mother, a bit frantic even though she had told her mother as they got in the car, "We don't have to rush." "What?" her mother had said. "We don't have to rush," Laura had repeated. The issue that day was her mother's pacemaker, which was due for a new battery. Laura thought she had everything all set, including lining up a technician to come to her mother's room to do some required lab work, but the technician had canceled at the last minute and suggested they try again next Wednesday, but next Wednesday was when her mother had a hair appointment, so now she had her mother in the car thinking they could just go to a lab and walk in. But how long would that take? Because Meredith needed her lunch. Because the puppy had eaten the turkey. She was stopped at a red light, lost in thought, trying to figure out what to do when the light turned green.

"It's green," her mother said.

There was the lab, up ahead. Maybe the line wouldn't be bad. She pulled in to the parking lot and told her mother to sit tight for a moment while she went in to see how busy it was.

"So you want me to get out?"

"No. Wait. I'll be right back."

"Okey-dokey."

She ran.

She ran back. There was only one person in line, but that could change in a flash if other people showed up, people who moved faster than an eighty-eight-year-old who said okey-dokey.

"All right. Let's go!" Laura said, and eventually her mother was safely back in her room, and Laura was walking into the house where Meredith was fine, just fine, watching a show on her iPad, and Laura was thinking what she was always thinking about Meredith, that this child was entirely dependent on her. As she'd said one day, saying out loud her constant, driving, suffocating thought, "Let's say Meredith is at school, and I'm in the shower, and I slip and fall and knock myself out and drown. Or a more likely scenario, someone crashes into me on the road. Whatever happens to me happens to me. But poor Meredith. If I'm not there to get her off the bus, everything she knows about the world is upended. 'Where is my mom to get me off the bus?' For her, it's not whether I'm unconscious or dead, it's 'Where is my mom to get me off the bus? She's always here.'"

WHEN DID THINGS become so anxious?

It's not as if Election Day 2016 had been the start of her worries. "It only takes one time, right?" Laura had been telling Brent about why he needed to close the garage door for as long as they'd been living in houses with garage doors. "It only takes one time for something to happen. Right? It probably won't happen. But one time, and you can't recover."

Or what she had been telling Emily since Emily was a teenager, to never, ever, ever get in a stranger's car, even at gunpoint, "because then you're dead. You always fight to get away before you're in the car." Also, "run in a zigzag pattern," and, if you're caught, start swinging. "All the vulnerable parts are right down the center of the body. Nose. Throat. Sternum. Personal parts."

She had always been self-protective and capable of worry, texting Brent, for instance, every time she went for a run about which path she was taking and which direction she was running. But any anxiety she had been feeling shifted into something more personal and menacing on November 9, 2015, when her president became someone who had held a campaign rally in South Carolina during which he seemed to mock a reporter with a disability. He had flailed his arms and contorted his face, and, making it worse, people were laughing. Laura hadn't liked Trump much to begin with, but that was when her disgust took off.

Who mocks someone with a disability? And it had built from there.

His attack on the family of a soldier who had been killed in Iraq. His feuds with other Gold Star families. His daily targets for belittling. His relentless divisiveness and fearmongering. These were not ways she wanted her president to behave, but what she was feeling went beyond just him. It was about the spreading effects of him. Or, on some days, what felt like the seepage of him. It was those laughing people. It was what he was unleashing, ever more visceral now to her, so much so that she could feel the danger moving into Georgia, into the cities, into the suburbs, up the highway and off at her exit, which one day, as she approached it with Meredith, was swarming with police cars.

"Holy shit. What is going *on*?" she said, pulling over.

There must have been eight of them. Cop cars were on the entrance and exit ramps. Cop cars were on the overpass.

"Did they find a dead body?"

Now cops were out of their cars and running.

She grabbed her phone to see if anything had been posted on the county sheriff's department page, and there it was:

****TRAFFIC ALERT**** We are getting reports of a COW on Ga. 400 southbound south of Peachtree Parkway.

Laura started laughing, and only laughed harder when she saw what someone had posted in response: "Was he on his way to Chick-fil-A?"

So it wasn't a murder. So maybe the danger hadn't arrived, yet.

"Good. Now I can speed down the highway because no one's around to stop me," she said, and hit the gas. She was on her way to the airport to pick up her sister, who was flying in to visit their mother. Rush hour traffic was building. Some dark clouds were moving in. Now, an hour later, Laura's sister in the car, those clouds burst open, not with rain but hail that kept getting bigger and bigger, bouncing off the car.

"Oh, shit. It's hailing. Now what do I do?"

"Get under a bridge," her sister said helpfully.

"There's no bridge!" Laura said, and as the hail kept beating down, she kept driving, thinking: *A hailstorm? It never hails here. How am I going to tell Brent the car was ruined by hail?* Now the phone was ringing. "Oh, hi," her mother said. "Are you home?" "No, we're still on the highway," Laura said over the sound of the storm. "What?" her mother said. Now the hail was slowing down. Now the hail was stopping. Now they were getting off the highway where there were no police cars or cows.

Now they were pulling in to the driveway and Laura was pressing the button to open the garage door.

"This is a really pretty house, Laura," her sister said.

AND IT WAS. She knew that. They all were pretty houses, including the one across the street that had the same floorplan as hers, the house whose owner had moved away and turned it into an Airbnb.

"Which house?" someone asked at a meeting of the Homeowners Association, during a discussion about neighborhood safety.

"It's on my street, at the end of the cul-de-sac," Laura said.

"We have an interesting story," one homeowner said, who lived one street over from Laura. "We share the same house number as the Airbnb. And we were out of town, and we had someone watching our dogs, and these people pulled in the driveway and barged in and said, 'We're here.' And they got real pushy and belligerent about it and almost pushed past her to get into the house."

"She said, 'No! You're not coming in!'" that house's co-owner said. "So it was a real mess, and it scared her. She called us and she was really upset. She said, 'I can't believe there's an Airbnb.' I said I didn't know it either."

"The thing is, when you have transient people like that, I would be concerned about all of the kids in the neighborhood," someone else said. "Who are these people? We don't know who these people are."

"One night I came home, somebody was riding my rear all the way through the neighborhood, and I turned in to my house, and they didn't get out of their car for a while, and then they did, and they were like sitting under the mailbox of that house, and then another car came, they got something and went in the house," Laura said about the Airbnb house. "Now it could have just been Uber Eats, but it totally sketched me out. It was just weird. Somebody sitting under the mailbox with a hoodie up, it was just weird. I mean I installed an alarm system, I've got three cameras on the outside of my house now because it just, you know, my husband's been deployed. It scares me. You know?"

"Other than the wrong address, what are other problems with the Airbnb?" someone asked.

"Well, they were using the amenities," someone said, mentioning the community pool.

"Cruising the neighborhood," someone else said.

"And there was a concern it was the people in the Airbnb that did the mailbox theft," someone else said.

"Like, I don't have any problem raising my girls to be afraid of that one creepy house in the neighborhood, but . . ."

"And new people in every other week, too . . ."

"And this is a family neighborhood. It's not an Airbnb neighborhood. It doesn't belong here."

It was late when the meeting ended, and most of the house lights in Pleasantville were off for the night, though not at the Airbnb. The light in the upstairs room that was the same as Emily's bedroom was still on, and so was the light in the room that was the same as Meredith's.

Who was in there?

The people at the Airbnb were always changing. The

longest to stay there was a woman named Liz, who had
lived at the Airbnb nearly a year. "I'll never forget it," she
said of her first time walking into the house. "All the
lights were on, it was bright and airy, and I went in the
living room, and it smelled like leather, and I thought,
'Where am I?' This is like heaven." Liz's bedroom was in
the room that in Laura's house was the equivalent of
Meredith's room, and one reason she had been able to
afford it was a deal she had cut with the owner to clean
rooms in between guests, so she knew more about who
had been in that house than anyone else.

"You never know who's coming," she said one day,
cleaning the room of someone who'd left the day before.
There was a man who hid a cat in his room, even though
pets weren't allowed. There was a couple from Florida
who'd met online and decided that a random house on a
cul-de-sac in Pleasantville would be where they would
first meet in person. They got in a vicious argument about
whether the man was cheating on the woman, and the
woman left, came back drunk, and was on the stairs
screaming and cussing while the man was putting his
hand over her mouth to quiet her. There were some men
who showed up in a moving truck, which worried Liz because she'd heard on the news about robbers emptying
Airbnbs of furniture, and also because the lock on her
bedroom door wasn't working. "What if they break in in
the middle of the night? What if they want to come in my
room? Yeah, that was scary."

Probably fifty people had stayed in the house over the
year Liz had been there, and the one who gave her the
most pause was the one she knew best, a woman who

had lived for months in the bedroom that in Laura's house was Emily's bedroom. That was the room Liz was cleaning because the woman had moved out the day before after being informed by the owner she had to go.

"She told me she came from a really well-to-do family. She said she got married, and they didn't like the guy, and they cut her off, and they disinherited her. She told me this husband drank a lot, and she had to bail him out of trouble. She said she had to divorce him," Liz said, relating what the woman had told her about how she came to be in the house, and there was more, a lot more, none of which added up to Liz. Worse, the more the woman told her, the less sense it made to her, and then one day she found the woman in the garage, crying and talking about how everyone was out to get her: lawyers, judges, investigators, and politicians, including the current governor of Georgia in his previous role as secretary of state.

Was any of it true? In fact, just before arriving at the house, the woman had been in jail for a little more than a year, according to a court file in a county about fifty miles away. She had been charged with impersonating a lawyer and had undergone a court-ordered competency evaluation by a psychologist who concluded "she was vague, difficulty [sic] to follow, and illogical, indicating possible thought disorder," and that she exhibited "what appear to be both paranoid and grandiose delusions." A judge took it a step further, declaring that she had "irrational, narcissistic, paranoid and grandiose delusions," after giving her a chance to testify at a hearing during which, according to a court transcript, she kicked off her testimony by saying, "Because the interviewing doctor has said, in her report, that my story was vague, difficult to follow and at points entirely illogical, my conclusions will follow logic models modus potem, modus totum, totus potum and potus potem." And it went on from there. She said she had met a man on a dating site who had begun cyberstalking her. She said he turned out to be a state investigator assigned to investigate her for impersonating a lawyer, that a mysterious surveillance app had been downloaded without her knowledge to her phone, and that another surveillance device was tracking her in her bedroom. She said that there had been a cover-up that stretched to the highest levels, and that a lot of people, important people, were in cahoots. She *was* a lawyer, she said. She *was* competent . . .

And eventually, she was in the house at the end of the cul-de-sac, after having been found guilty and released from jail, and now, after many months there, she was packing up to move out because, in her telling, she had inadvertently left a makeup stain on a wall and the owner wanted fifty dollars for it to be cleaned. "I was blessed here," she said as she packed, grateful for what the months in the house had given her. She had arrived in Pleasantville with only two pans, one pot, one pair of blue jeans, two shirts, and two sets of underwear that while in jail she had learned made a handy substitute for hair curlers if you were dressing to go to court, and she was leaving with a car stuffed to the gills, including two bottles of water she had grabbed from a refrigerator and a loaf of slightly moldy bread. So it had been a good run for her, no trouble, a chance for recovery, and before getting in her car she took a last look around. A neighbor was across the street, coming toward her. "Hi," she called, waving, and then realized the neighbor's focus was on two deer on her lawn. "Beautiful, beautiful, beautiful," she said to the neighbor. "Look at them. We all share the world," but the neighbor was only interested in making clapping sounds until the deer ran away, and then the neighbor went inside, and the woman left, and the room that was in the same place as Emily's room was vacant, and a day later Liz was cleaning the room and putting out seven Hershey's Kisses on the bed for the next arrival and saying of the neighborhood, "I tell you it's the most beautiful place."

Beautiful.

Heaven.

Or, as Laura's sister said after a day there, "Like where the perfect family lives."

And Laura thought so too, but that didn't mean it didn't need a hammer under the mattress and a can of wasp spray on the nightstand.

It wasn't just the weird vibes from the Airbnb. A couple of months before, just a few neighborhoods away in a subdivision of beige houses and maple saplings, the skies one afternoon filled with the racket of two black helicopters hovering over a house of a twenty-one-year-old man plotting to attack the White House, the Washington Monument, the Lincoln Memorial, a Washington-area synagogue, and the Statue of Liberty. "A martyrdom operation" was how undercover agents said the man had described his plans to them, and as fantastical as they might have seemed, he'd been arrested trying to buy semiautomatic rifles, an antitank weapon, and grenades.

And now came word from Emily's university that a student the night before had come out of one of the bars in a popular downtown area, arranged for an Uber, gotten into a car that pulled up, and been driven away by a man who wasn't an Uber driver. Instead, he activated childproof locks so she couldn't get out and then stabbed her so many times, in so many places, there was barely any blood left in her when her body was found.

And how many times had Emily been in those bars, at that intersection, waiting for an Uber, Laura thought when she heard. Run zigzag, she had said. Go for the vulnerable parts, she had said. But she had never said anything about childproof locks. She felt sick to her stomach. She looked at the tracker app on her phone and called Emily.

"I saw you over by Pier One and Target," she said.

"Yeah," Emily said.

"What'd you get?" Laura asked.

NOW IT WAS Brent on the phone, calling from Jerusalem.

"How are you?"

"Tired," Laura said. "The drive last night, unfricking real. We're trying to get on to 400 and see like six to eight cop cars, blue lights, driving the wrong way up the 400 ramps, like driving up the on ramps, I'm like what is going on? So I quickly push into their Twitter feed. Cow on the highway."

"Cow?"

"Great drive down," Laura went on. "A little overcast. But not bad. As soon as we pull out of the parking garage, it starts fricking hailing. And my sister's like, 'Pull over! Go to an underpass!' Where? Really? Where am I going to do that? It really was hailing. I about lost my mind."

A pause.

"Did it mess up the car at all?" Brent asked.

One thing Laura had learned when Brent had been in Iraq was the importance of saying only so much on the phone and in emails. He would let her know when he was about to go out on any kind of a mission, and as his deployment continued, and the first soldier was killed, and then the second, she asked him not to say anything about going out until he had come back.

Now, with him away again in Jerusalem, she was always happy to hear from him and always ready to describe her days as if she were a character in a sitcom, but the last thing she was going to do was tell him the true reality of those days, that they were closing in on her.

If anything made her vulnerable to the fearmongering of a president, it was this. The fears she had, fears that someone like Donald Trump could take advantage of, weren't about external things like his wall, but were about the internal fears of someone wondering about a life's meaning and a life's worth. They were the most exploitable fears of all. One day, talking about Meredith— Meredith who didn't speak, Meredith who would be hard pressed to understand why a dime is worth more than a penny because a penny is bigger than a dime, Meredith who would never be able to live any kind of independent life—Laura had said, "What impact does Meredith Cummings have on the world? Does her life have any impact at all?"

But of course she wasn't only talking about Meredith.

Right before Brent left, she had tried to bring up this feeling of hollowness that was growing in her, saying to him one night as they were getting ready for bed, "What's the point? Of anything? I'm tired of the struggle, and the stress, and what's the point of this when we're just going to die anyway, no matter what?"

Instead of saying anything back, he'd left the room, and when she found him later, he was downstairs at the kitchen table.

"The things you said, that's what my dreams are about," he'd said.

"I'm sorry," she'd said.

"It's okay," he'd said. "It's all right. I'm just going to sit here awhile. If I go upstairs, I'm just going to have a dream."

Soon after that was when he suggested she get a puppy, and now, walking the puppy one afternoon, hurrying because she still had to get to the pharmacy to pick up some pills for her mother, she described her own version of the darkness that Brent had hinted at:

"It's nothing. It's utter nothing," she said. Nothing to see. Nothing to hear. Nothing to feel. "Just nothing," she said, and then said such a place was becoming attractive to her.

"I *want* to be there," she said.

Off to the pharmacy.

Recently, more and more, she was finding herself thinking about the pills her mother had been prescribed, all of them stashed in Laura's pantry for safekeeping. The tramadol. The hydrocodone.

If she took the pills, would it be like going to sleep?

No. No. At least not while Meredith was alive. No.

Home now, with a few minutes to spare. Once again, she had gotten everything done. She sat on the front porch, waiting. She was sinking, she knew it, just as she knew that in a few days she'd be better and back to believing what she said now as an act of persuasion: "I may not leave a legacy in this world. But making lives easier, that helps me to have a purpose."

She looked at the fitness tracker she wore. Twenty thousand steps.

Where had she gone?

Here came the bus.

The doors opened.

"Hey, Mer!"

CHAPTER 4

BEFORE BRENT WENT to Jerusalem, he was outside one afternoon when he saw his nextdoor neighbor. He waved cordially, just being a neighbor, and once again, through no fault of his own, his life was about to take on another complication.

His neighbor was Michael Owens, who had one of the smoothest and greenest front lawns in all of Pleasant-ville. This was no small achievement, because Michael had been in a wheelchair for a couple of decades, the re-sult of an accident that had left him paralyzed with quad-riplegia. He did what he could with the limited movement he had, but he depended on a lawn man, who also took care of Brent's lawn, which was not among the nicest be-cause of a patch that never seemed to get green. Brent thought that the lawn man must have overfertilized it, but Laura had her own theory, that maybe it went all the way back to the previous owner of the house who'd had a bad drinking problem, so bad his family moved out and left him alone in that big house with his liquor, and then he lost his job, and then he ran out of money, and then he sold off his furniture, and then the power got shut off, and then things got so awful for him that neighbors were offering him wood scraps to heat his house. Maybe it was *more* than drinking, Laura said. Maybe there were drugs involved. Maybe he owed money to his dealers, a lot of money, and to send a message to him that he better pay up, the dealers hired the lawn man to poison the lawn.

"Huh?" Brent said, unable to contain a look that came over him sometimes.

"You don't have to be an asshole about it," Laura said.

"I think he just made a mistake," Brent said, not saying what he was really thinking, that every so often Pleasantville could feel as baffling as Iraq.

They had been on their front porch when they'd had that conversation, Brent's favorite place in all the house, but now he was in his deficient front yard when he heard Michael and called out to him.

"Good afternoon, Colonel," Michael called back, and soon they were talking about the squirrels that were trying to get into both their attics and Brent was saying that a few hours earlier he'd been on his back deck with his old BB gun, taking aim at one.

His intention had been to scare it away, nothing more, not that hitting it with a BB gun would have done much damage. His old gun wasn't going to hurt anything, which was fine with him because the last thing he wanted to do was kill a squirrel, but instead of telling Michael that, he said the problem he was having was that when he had leveled the gun to aim it, the squirrel had heard the BBs rolling around and knew something was coming.

"These little squirrels are smart," he said. "I have to get smarter."

"I got no sympathy for them," Michael said.

"I have to be a better sniper," Brent said.

"I got a high-powered BB gun, and I got no problem if you want to cull the squirrels," Michael said.

"Sure," Brent said, again cordially, hoping that would be the end of it, but a few hours later Michael was rolling into Brent's garage and handing over the gun, saying, "I don't need to show *you* how to use it."

This was true. Brent knew how to use handguns, shotguns, single-shot rifles, semiautomatic rifles, and machine guns, not to mention RPGs and mortars.

And he knew what weapons could do, and not only from being a soldier. He was a hunter, and a good one. But he had never killed a squirrel, or had wanted to.

Why hadn't he just told Michael the truth, that he didn't want to kill something just to kill something?

Don't lie. It had been drilled into him by his father, by his ROTC program in college, and by the Army itself. "I have a hard time *not* telling the truth," he insisted, although he also knew that complete honesty for him was still a work in progress. Just the other morning, he had woken before Laura, gone downstairs to let the dog out, and in the first dim light of morning had seen a mess from the dog on the white carpet. He had made coffee. Then he had drunk the coffee. Then he had tied his shoes. He had needed to get going to an appointment he couldn't be late for. He'd made a second cup of coffee. "All right. What am I going to do about the dog shit?" he'd thought. There wasn't time to drag out the steam cleaner, not after that second cup, so maybe he should run upstairs, wake Laura and say, "Hey, I'm leaving. Tucker shit on the floor." Or maybe just text her that. But instead what he had texted was, "Sorry I didn't let him out. He was just sleeping and I left." The mess had stayed where it was for Laura to discover, and it had worked out, because when he'd gotten home that night, the carpet was clean.

"So I didn't *lie*," was how he justified it. "I didn't share information."

So he hadn't shared information, and now he hadn't shared information with Michael, and he was disappointed in himself because as he put it later, still thinking about it, "I didn't have the courage to say to him, 'Thank you, but I don't want to kill a squirrel.' It bothers me that I didn't have the courage to say the truth."

Courage and truth. Frustration and anger. There was so much to work on in order to be a good person.

"Okay, thanks," was what he did say to Michael. "I'll get it back to you."

"No rush," Michael said, wheeling away, and after he was gone Laura asked Brent what he had wanted.

"He gave me this," Brent said, showing her the BB gun and explaining what he was supposed to do with it.

"Are you going to kill a squirrel?" she asked.

"I don't really want to kill a squirrel," he said.

He leaned the BB gun in a corner of the kitchen.

He wasn't going to kill a squirrel. Instead, he was going to have some dinner cooked in one of those misaligned ovens, and then he was going to go to bed, and then he was going to have that dream.

MEANWHILE, MICHAEL ROLLED AWAY, glad to have helped a neighbor.

The BB gun wasn't his only gun, far from it. As he rolled along one of the quietest streets in all of Pleasantville, he had a handgun strapped to his right ankle and another stashed in a mesh basket under the seat of his wheelchair. He passed Brent's mailbox, which by neighborhood code was the same color and shape as every other mailbox. He wheeled up his own driveway and into his house, where, locked in a gun safe, were more handguns and rifles, along with spare magazines and stacks of boxed ammunition.

"Think about it like this," he said, explaining how, because of his physical condition, he couldn't help but think about it.

If someone broke in, it would take the police five to eight minutes to get to his house, according to his calculations, and if someone came at him and tipped him over and he couldn't get to the handgun in his basket, he could reach for the one on his ankle, and such were the constant thoughts of a wheelchair-bound man with quadriplegia—a "quad" was how Michael described himself—all because of what had happened when he was twenty-eight years old, half his life ago. He shouldn't be alive. He knew that. He knew it was because of God's most merciful will that he was alive, just as he knew it was God's most punishing will that the sinner he used to be climbed a pine tree in his backyard one afternoon to clear away some dead branches. There was so much he could remember. He was living in another part of Georgia then with his second wife, whom he had married two weeks before. It was four o'clock. It was ninety degrees. He was about sixty feet up. He was wearing red shorts and a white sleeveless muscle shirt. He was thirsty and remembered thinking he should have been drinking more water. There were some things he didn't remember after reaching for a branch, feeling dizzy, and passing out. A neighbor who watched it happen told him later that he had dropped in a dead dive and hit the ground facefirst. The EMTs told him they had found his front teeth in the grass and did their best to stick them back in. He didn't remember that, either, but he did remember that one of the EMTs was named Jerry and they had a conversation in the ambulance as he came more fully into consciousness.

"What happened?"

"You fell. A long way."

"I can't feel anything. Jerry, am I gonna die?"

"You don't look good."

He remembered starting to feel pain as the ambulance took him to a hospital, particularly in his neck, and that the smooth road began to feel like it was turning into cobblestones.

Teeth, hanging. Jaw, broken. Tongue, almost entirely bitten through.

"You cut your spinal cord in half," a doctor said the next day, showing Michael X-rays.

His new wife was there, next to the hospital bed.

"How long until he's up and around and back to his old self?" his wife asked.

"You don't understand," the doctor said.

Those words hung in the air.

"It's only by the grace of God he's alive," the doctor went on.

"GOOD MORNING, COLONEL," Michael called out one day to Brent, who was moving stiffly. "How are you, sir?"

"I broke my rib," Brent called over.

"How?" Michael asked.

"Oh, I got in an argument with a Navy SEAL," Brent said.

"Are you serious?" Michael asked.

"Had to put him in his place," Brent said.

"Are you *serious*?" Michael asked again.

"No. I wish I was. I think that would be a better story," Brent said.

"Well, I was gonna say," Michael said, laughing, and then stopped. "I'm not laughing at your misfortune."

"No, go ahead," Brent said, and then told him the embarrassing truth: that he had been away on a hunting trip, had gotten locked out of his cabin, didn't have a key, had the bright idea to hoist himself up onto a balcony where there was a door he thought was unlocked, saw a rickety chair, stood on that rickety chair, and was about to grab on to the balcony and pull himself up when a chair leg broke.

"And I came down horizontal and broke my tenth rib," Brent said.

"I am so sorry," Michael said.

"No, don't be sorry. I was a dummy. I deserved it," Brent said.

"Knock the wind out of you pretty good?" Michael said.

"Oh, it blacked me out," Brent said. "I mean, have you ever broken a rib?"

"How far did you fall?" Michael said, not answering.

"About five, five and a half feet," Brent said.

"Thank the good Lord it was nothing worse," Michael said.

"I know. Exactly," Brent said, and if it didn't occur to him that he was talking to a man who had fallen sixty feet from a tree and had been in a wheelchair since, it was because of what happens with neighbors, how familiar they can become with each other, even if what they know amounts to nothing more than the revelations of polite conversation.

In Brent's case, that meant always saying thank you when Michael would thank him for his years of military service and never giving any indication of the scream that escaped from him every night as he fell asleep.

In Michael's case, it meant never giving any indication that being out in his driveway was the far end of a daily routine that began when his alarm went off at two-thirty A.M. First came the matter of getting out of bed and into his chair. Then came an hour-and-a-half-long process that those with quadriplegia simply call their bowel program, followed by propelling himself an inch or two at a time across a transfer board into the shower, followed by all it takes to dry off and to get dressed. Socks were relatively easy. Jeans could be diabolical. But at last Michael was ready for the rest of his day, feeling once again fortunate that the particular bone he broke, his C7, had allowed a life in which he was at least able to move his head, neck, and shoulders and had limited use of his arms and hands.

"How are you feeling now?" he asked Brent.

"Better. A lot better. Thanks," Brent said, and soon their conversation came to its polite end and Michael was getting in his van to run some errands.

Electric ramp down.

He rolled onto the lift.

Electric ramp up.

He maneuvered the chair back and forth and back and forth until he was next to the driver's seat.

Every morning, he lifted weights to help with what came next, pushing himself up from the chair and swinging his one hundred sixty pounds of dead weight into the driver's seat, all of it done by arm and shoulder strength because of the uselessness of his hips and legs.

Into the driver's seat now, his face reddened, a little out of breath.

One last thing to do.

Years before, just after he got out of the hospital, his wife at the time took him to get a pedicure, and in the midst of it, with no warning of what was about to happen, his right leg spasmed and his foot shot forward into the nail technician's chest. "He's paralyzed, and he kicked me," he remembered her screaming. "I'm so sorry. I didn't mean it," he'd said, but she kept screaming. "He's possessed," she screamed, "he's possessed," and even after twenty-seven subsequent years of indignities, something about that remained especially humiliating.

Now, he grabbed a bungee cord and strapped his leg to the metal base of the car seat.

There.

Ready.

WHY DOES HE call me Colonel? Brent would wonder. *Why does he call me sir? Why doesn't he call me Brent?*

It was a type of politeness that could seem overly genteel, formal even, between neighbors, and yet Brent recognized that Michael, like him, was most comfortable in a world of courtesies and rules. They had that in common, and other things as well. They were about the same age. They were both born in the Deep South. They both loved dogs and shooting guns. They both had daughters, although in Michael's case, his daughter was grown and gone and he hadn't spoken to her in a decade. Their estrangement was a source of pain to Michael because, like Brent, he knew the importance of a father in a child's life, even a grown child, and that was one more thing he and Brent had in common, dead fathers who remained constant voices in their sons' heads.

"You're going to love her," Brent's father told him the day Meredith was born, and there was no way to count how many times Brent had heard those words since.

"Stand on your feet and pray on your knees," Michael's father said, and how many times since his accident had Michael thought of the wheelchair-bound version of that?

"Love, Dad," was how Brent's father ended every email to him while Brent was in Iraq, and Brent had saved every one.

"Hey, your mother's got breakfast ready," Michael's father would say when Michael was a boy, waking him up before sunrise. "You wanna run around with me today?" And off they would go.

"Dad," Brent wrote to his father at the end of one of the worst days of all in his war, just before he began having his dream. "Our luck ran out today, lost two. Three continue to fight for their lives. Lost count of the enemy dead. Still adding to the number, this is unbelievable."

"Hi Brent, I had just come in from working on the project and had checked my computer at the kitchen table when your 'Luck Ran Out' message came in. That news was really tough to take. I simply could not reply. I'm so sorry for you and your troops and heartsick over this loss of those two fine men. I pray that the other three will recover," his father wrote back, and then, a few hours later, wrote again: "My thinking is this crucible will breed a new type of leader for our country in the years to come and we will be stronger as a result. The people that will rise up and lead will understand the stakes better . . ."

The email went on for a while longer, but when Brent wrote back it was to mention the cancer his father had been fighting while Brent was away in Iraq. "I'm sorry about your hair, you went so long with it," he wrote. "How long do you stay on this drug? I assume it will come back once you stop?"

"I think it's going to be a close race between my hair and your homecoming. I think the hair will not make it that long. It is going quick now. Oh well," his father had replied, and there weren't many emails after that because soon Brent was home and his father was dying slowly and steadily in front of him.

If only Brent could get that last image out of his mind, his father choking on that last can of Ensure, but he could not—just as Michael couldn't stop hearing the last words his own father had said to him: "Don't leave."

It was the final act of a life that lasted seventy years and whose most generous moment had come just before Michael had been born.

His father was living just south of Atlanta at that point. He had grown up in poverty in south Georgia, dropped out of school in seventh grade to help with the family farm, lost part of a leg when he was clearing stumps and a saw got out of control, eventually gave up on farming, moved to a little box of a house near Atlanta that he bought for nine thousand dollars, ran a gas station for a while, became a florist for a while, loaded and unloaded freight trucks for a while, did whatever it took without complaint, and was married to a woman who had suffered through several miscarriages and whose brother-in-law was down in Florida one day, eating breakfast at a diner, when he heard a girl at the next table starting to cry.

She was sixteen years old, three months pregnant, and didn't know what she was going to do.

Two weeks later, the girl was living in Georgia in the smallest bedroom of the little house. Six months after that she gave birth to Michael, and a few days after that she disappeared, and Michael became the adopted son of a man who taught him how to shell peas, how to fish, how to shoot a gun, how to plant a pecan tree. With Michael's help, his father planted a pecan tree in the front yard, and in the backyard a peach tree, an apple tree, a fig tree, and two catalpa trees. The catalpa trees would produce worms that Michael and his father would sell as bait as a way to make money after his father retired. They would sell crickets and red wiggler worms, too, stuffed into cups that he and his father would get from a factory in downtown Atlanta, driving there in a chocolate-brown Ford LTD stained yellow in the interior from the cigarettes his father was always smoking. Then on Sundays was church, always church, Michael between his parents with his own Bible that he kept next to his bed. His parents had Bibles on their nightstands, too, and there was a fourth Bible—the main Bible, they called it—on top of the TV. We're a family that believes in four things, his father would tell him, leaving no room for ambivalence. The Bible. The Constitution. The First Amendment. And the Second Amendment, which was created to protect the First.

Weekends were always so simple, and then came weekdays, when his father was at work and things were more complicated.

Inside the little house, bottles of vodka were everywhere, clumsily hidden in kitchen cabinets and behind beds. Michael never knew the source of his mother's sadness, perhaps the miscarriages, perhaps something else, but whatever the reasons were, she was a drunk, and sometimes a violent one.

"I'm not drunk!" she would scream at him.

"I'm not drunk!" she would scream at his father.

He stayed outside as much as he could. When he got off the school bus, he would walk heel to toe, heel to toe, every step of the way, to take as long as possible. One warm evening, instead of eating inside with his parents, he took his dinner outside and was just settling in under the pecan tree when his mother was flying at him and grabbing the plate and sailing it through the yard, and then his father was next to her, saying, "That's enough!" and pulling her inside. He didn't know what happened next because he left. He was fourteen years old, and he walked several miles to a friend's house and stayed there until his father came to him.

"I'm sorry about all of this," he remembers his father saying, and then he was home again, where he remained for another four years.

Eventually, after Michael had moved out, his mother stopped drinking and became as nice a person as he'd forever wanted her to be. She and his father stayed married, and after he died, she lived in the house by herself for the rest of her life, keeping to herself and in spite of her age doing all of the chores, including the one that killed her. She was replacing a furnace filter. The filter was part of an ancient gas furnace with a large opening in the floor for the air intake, and she had removed the covering to the intake and from what the police surmised was leaning over when she fell in headfirst, became stuck and suffocated. How long she had been there no one could say. Her life by then had become so solitary and circumscribed that she didn't have many visitors, but a neighbor happened to notice that the door to the house was open, went inside calling her name, and discovered at the end of a hallway a sight that Michael was still seeing a decade after her death.

"Just her feet, sticking in the air," Michael said. It was an awful image. It was a sad image, and a lonesome one, and it stayed with him as one more damning lesson about life, though not as much as his final image of his father, which cut into him more than anything else.

His fall out of the pine tree was still two years away at that point. He was away on a hunting trip but had a funny feeling that he should see his father, so he packed up and went to visit a man who was always there waiting for him, seated in the living room and dressed for the day, his artificial leg with its scuffed wooden foot always strapped on even though he had nowhere to go. Michael got to the house just after an ambulance was pulling away. His father had fallen from bed, and things went downhill quickly. Now he was in a hospital bed, sick with so many things, emphysema especially, gasping for breath. A nurse was there, too, who told Michael he should take a break and go get some rest.

"Don't leave," his father gasped.

It's okay, the nurse said. His father needed to sleep.

"Don't leave."

He left.

Soon after that, before he could get back, his father was dead; two years after that, he was falling from the pine tree; and some years after that, his third wife, Ann, was asking him a question. Of all the things that had happened to him in his difficult life, she asked, what had been the hardest to live with?

"It's not the wheelchair," he told her. "It's regret."

———

HE MET ANN eight years after his accident. His second marriage was long over by then, he had just undergone his seventh surgery, and as he lay in his hospital room, he heard someone calling his name. He was on his stomach and turned to see who it was, which was no easy task for anyone with quadriplegia and especially someone with a fresh incision that had been closed with fifty-one staples. He saw a technician he knew, and next to her was Ann. She had red hair, and the way the light from a window was backlighting her, Michael thought she was glowing.

"Michael, right?" she said, reading his name off a chart.

"Yes."

"Can I get you anything?"

She changed his dressings. She changed his IV bags. "She would make sure my JP drains were empty," was Michael's memory of that first meeting, marveling at how tender something like that could seem. "She would make sure my staples weren't bleeding." She was a weekend nurse, and as her shift was ending on Sunday, even though he was in the care of another nurse that day, she stopped in to say goodbye.

The following weekend she was back, and after she changed his dressings, he took a chance and asked her if she might be feeling about him what he was feeling about her, because at that point in his life what did he have to lose? He was alone in life, talking with no one other than in prayer with God, whom he could hear castigating him for everything he had done up to the moment he reached for that branch. "I told you," he heard God say in those conversations. "You didn't listen. I tried to tell you. So here you go, dumbass."

Was more pain even possible?

So he asked, and the answer Ann gave him marked the moment when his thinking about his accident shifted, that it wasn't punishment after all. That he hadn't fallen from the tree so much as God had pushed him from the tree, and had given him quadriplegia, and had provided him with infections and fevers and nausea and blisters and bedsores and skin so raw that he would wake to blood-streaked sheets, and had gifted him with two dark days when he was so depressed he thought of killing himself and, finally, the opportunity for this seventh surgery, all of it so that he could meet this woman who was telling him yes, she was feeling it too.

One year later, freshly married, they were moving into their house.

"This was always the goal," Michael said one day, driving through the neighborhood, just so happy, and it was the same for Ann. "A quadriplegic?" her mother had said when Ann told her about Michael, but after two turbulent marriages, followed by a relationship with a man who threw coffee at her and blackened one of her eyes, she was feeling a kind of peace with Michael she hadn't expected in her life.

The years went by. They fell into a pleasing routine. From that childhood house to this house, this had been Michael's journey, and he was grateful for it.

July 2015 now, and new neighbors, the Cummings family, were moving in next door.

"Hi, Colonel," Michael began saying.

November 9, 2016, now, and Michael was waking up at two-thirty A.M.

The night before, he and Ann had gone to sleep upset about how the presidential election was turning out. Since his first vote for president in 1984, when he voted for Ronald Reagan, Michael had voted for Republicans, but this election wasn't about anything as simple as party loyalty. His vote this time hadn't been for Donald Trump. It had been against Hillary Clinton, because he knew that no matter what she might have promised, she was going to take his guns away, every one of them, even the shotgun his father had given him when he was twelve. He despised her for this, and when he had gone to sleep, it was with the understanding that when he woke up, she would have been elected his next president, he would soon be unable to protect himself, and the feeling of imminent threat he had felt as a boy would be returning.

"Do you want to turn on the TV?" he asked Ann.

"Let's just get it over with," Ann said.

On came the TV and an image of Hillary Clinton looking somber.

"What is this?" Ann said. "I'm very confused."

"Baby, I don't know," Michael said.

They kept watching, and now here came the numbers.

"Trump won!" Michael hollered.

"What?" Ann said. "What?"

"Trump won!" he continued hollering. "Trump won! Trump won!"

CHAPTER 5

IN JERUSALEM, BRENT was living in the same apartment he had lived in once before, during an earlier deployment that had ended on June 16, 2015, which happened to be the day Donald Trump had declared his presidential candidacy. Brent had missed the beginning of the announcement when Trump had descended on that golden escalator, but as he'd sat on a duffel bag in the empty apartment, waiting for his ride to the airport and his flight home, he had listened to the rest of it, including the part about the wall, the "great wall," the "great, great wall" Trump was promising to build between the United States and Mexico. *What a joke,* Brent had thought, and now it was three years later, Trump was tweeting, "Wow highest Poll Numbers in the history of the Republican Party. That includes Honest Abe Lincoln and Ronald Reagan," and Brent was six thousand miles away from Pleasantville and feeling homesick.

He called home. It was a video call so he could see

everyone. There was Meredith, holding the cat and smiling her slight smile.

"I saw you swimming yesterday," Brent said to her. "Did you have fun?"

No answer.

"Oh look!" he said. "There's Mittens!"

Silence.

"Did you have fun, Mer?"

More silence, and then he heard Laura say, "Oh, Mer, it's all over your shirt. Ugh. Mer, you cannot pick the cat up. Every time you pick the cat up, it pees. No more picking up the cat."

"Stupid cat," he said, laughing, as Laura shouted, "No!"

He saw Laura running toward Emily, who was opening the door to put the cat outside.

"No!" Laura shouted again. "The hawk is out there!"

He stared, watching.

"All right," Laura finally said, picking up the phone.

"All right," he said.

More silence.

"Love you," he said.

"Love you too," he heard Laura and Emily both say.

He wasn't sure who hit the disconnect button.

Maybe Meredith.

A SATURDAY NOW. Saturdays in Jerusalem were the worst for him, and he had a lot of them to get through before he would be home.

Weekdays, on the other hand, were good because of

his job, a year-long assignment that would be his last in
the Army before going home to retire. He was helping to
run a program that involved training Palestinian Authority security forces in the West Bank—the Palestinian
territory between Israel and Jordan that Israel has occupied since the 1967 war. It was a program funded by the
U.S. State Department and run day to day by a multina-
tional staff headed by a three-star U.S. Army general, all
in the hope of improving security in the West Bank and
Israel by professionalizing the Palestinian forces, a para-
military organization with some forty thousand members, by teaching them things such as crowd control
tactics based on the rule of law and human rights.

But then came the weekend, when he was on his own
with nothing to do but walk around and see the reality
of what Jerusalem was, rather than what it might be if
the tensions and grievances that defined it were to suddenly go away. There were advantages to being an out-
sider. Brent knew that. When he was out walking, he
could enter Palestinian neighborhoods in Jerusalem that
Israelis would never go to. But there were disadvantages,
too, especially the lonesomeness that began for him at
sundown on Friday, when much of Jerusalem shut down
for twenty-four hours for the Jewish Sabbath, followed
by Saturday, when the stillness and silence were so complete it made him want to keep in motion as much as possible.

From Iraq to Pleasantville, the dream kept following
him. He wished he could admire its persistence. He just
wanted it to go away.

Now, wondering on this Saturday whether he had

screamed in his sleep and, if he had, who might have heard him, he boiled some water, made a cup of instant coffee, and looked in the refrigerator. Ketchup. Mayonnaise. Salad dressing. Two bags of cookies. He checked the freezer. A couple of breaded chicken cutlets and half a bag of French fries. He hadn't had time to shop, and the stores were closed until sundown, so he headed outside, past a field of olive trees, down a steep hill, and into Jerusalem's Old City, which was being guarded by armed Israeli border police.

The Jewish quarter was shuttered, but the Christian and Muslim quarters were open, and the narrow passageways that Brent pushed through were jammed with tourists headed toward the Church of the Holy Sepulchre, regarded as the site of Jesus Christ's crucifixion and resurrection.

Just before the final passageway to the church, Brent veered to the right, away from all of the people who would soon be in tears as they ran their hands over Christ's tomb, and a few steps later he was walking into the Al-Zohour Barber Shop.

"*Shou akhbarak,*" he called out in Arabic and looked at all of the people waiting. "How many, Mohammed?"

"Maybe one," Mohammed said.

"*Na'am?*" Brent said. Yes?

"*Na'am,*" Mohammed said.

"*Habibi,*" Brent said and took a seat.

"*Chai?*" Mohammed asked.

"*Na'am. Shukran,*" Brent said—yes, thank you—and as he waited for the tea, he picked up a copy of the *Jerusalem Post,* which had several stories on the front page about the latest battles between Hamas, a Palestinian national organization the U.S. has labeled a terrorist organization, and the Israel Defense Forces, or IDF.

HAMAS FIRES 30 ROCKETS AT ISRAEL'S SOUTH; IDF STRIKES 80 TARGETS IN GAZA was one headline.

He put the paper down. Here came the tea, served on a tray with sugar and fresh mint leaves, and Brent drank it while Mohammed finished with one customer, brushed off the chair, and welcomed the next customer in line, a huge man who removed his shirt and undershirt and settled his bare back against the vinyl. It was a warm, sweaty day, and when he was done, Brent took his place and closed his eyes as Mohammed cut his hair, applied some shaving cream, opened a straight razor, and scraped that razor with a barber's confidence along Brent's soft neck.

Where next?

Sometimes on Saturdays, he walked around downtown Jerusalem, past the building where he worked. There was a plaque out front with the words DONALD J. TRUMP PRESIDENT etched into it, and he marveled at the tourists, some on their way to the Old City to run their hands over Christ's tomb, who would stop and run their hands over Trump's name.

Sometimes he went into the Palestinian neighborhoods of East Jerusalem, to a butcher shop he had found one day when he was walking around the mobbed and chaotic streets that felt so different from the Jewish parts of Jerusalem.

Always, though, he ended up back in his apartment sooner than he wanted to, to wait out the hours until the Sabbath was over.

"What'd you do today?" Laura asked when he called.

"Pretty much nothing. I went to this butcher I like who's a good guy."

He waited for her to say something.

"So. Losh kebab from him," he said.

"All right," she said.

"Lonely day," he said.

His apartment came with a big outdoor roof deck, and that's where he headed now to take in the view.

There was the Old City, home to the Western Wall, the holiest place in Judaism, the Dome of the Rock, where the Prophet Muhammad is said to have ascended to heaven, and the Church of the Holy Sepulchre.

And just beyond it, to the east of where he had been walking, was the security wall running between Jerusalem and the West Bank, a concrete wall that was thirty feet high and ten feet thick.

A separation wall, necessary for security, was how it was referred to by Israelis, who had begun erecting it in 2002 to control Palestinian access out of the West Bank and into Israel, after a particularly violent period known as the Second Intifada. The wall was four hundred forty miles long, the distance between Washington, D.C., and Boston, and it was as high as the wall Trump was trying to build between the U.S. and Mexico.

A wall of segregation, of annexation, of apartheid was what Palestinians called it.

Life in this place felt so different, Brent thought, taking in the view. If the U.S. was fracturing, this was what came next.

It wasn't fracturing. It was fractured.

——

OF ALL THE THINGS the wall had been called, no one had ever called it "great, great," as Donald Trump was calling his wall, or for that matter even "great." Instead, it was a hulking, ever-present reminder of what can happen when violence and fears of violence overtake a place, as Brent had learned from getting to know two women who lived on opposite sides of the wall. One was a Palestinian woman named Tamara. The other was an Israeli woman named Rinat. Both were forty-four years old, both had grown up within a few miles of each other, and that was where their similarities ended.

Early one morning, Brent parked a few feet from the wall, waiting for Tamara to emerge. She was a co-worker of his whose list of Palestinian contacts went up to the highest levels of the Palestinian Authority. A Palestinian herself, she lived with her parents and brother on the Palestinian side of the wall, just beyond Bethlehem in the Palestinian Christian town of Beit Sahour, and for more than a decade, she had been getting to work through a checkpoint controlled by armed Israelis and overrun at times by the thousands of Palestinians with daytime work permits who move into Jerusalem through a series of barred chutes that the Israelis call control measures and the Palestinians call cages.

Here she came now, and when she climbed into Brent's car, she gave no indication of how dehumanizing she found the process of having to go through a wall. Instead, she simply said hello, and they headed out of Jerusalem for a meeting.

"Your phone or something is ringing," Brent said.

"Yeah. Mm-hmm," Tamara said, looking at the number and deciding to ignore it. She was on her phone constantly, if not talking then reading on it. This day, it was a story about a mass shooting in the U.S. in which eleven people had been killed at a synagogue, and Tamara said to Brent, "I read this morning in comments on social media that the guy who attacked the synagogue in Pittsburgh, that it was because of Trump's policies."

"Well, it was because of his rhetoric, is what people are saying," Brent said.

"No, this is stupid," Tamara said of such an explanation. "This is stupid. I think."

"Well, I don't know," Brent said, reminding her of the demonstration by white supremacists and neo-Nazis in Charlottesville, Virginia, and what Trump had said afterward. "I mean it's always been easy for a politician to say 'I don't like that,' or 'That's un-American, and it's intolerable.' But he didn't say that. A young woman was killed, and there was a lot of violence, and he said, 'Well, there's bad people on both sides.' It's just been very easy for politicians to say, 'Hey, I don't align with white supremacists,' but he didn't, and that's what people are saying, that he allowed this event to occur because he didn't condemn it. And people think by not condemning it, it gives it a little bit of authority, and then this guy does something like this. Tragically."

"I don't know," Tamara said. "It's easy to say 'because of President Trump.' It's the easiest thing." She paused for a moment, trying to figure out how to explain what she meant. "As an American, for *you,* you have not experienced how it feels when other people take advantage of you, when other people oppress you, when you live your life with uncertainty and there is no security, there is no safety, there is no future, there is no nothing. So because of the American way, you are protected. And the way you are raised, it's like you are in this bubble, a protected bubble, and you look at 'the other' as another human peer, you know? A human being. But the other is *not* a human being. The other is there to kill you. The other is there to take advantage of you, to rape your women and to steal you. And I think this is how Trump sees it."

"I understand what you're saying," Brent said, but Tamara knew he didn't, that he couldn't, because he didn't have a life that in any way included things such as the things she didn't have except as wishes.

There were so many things she wished for, as she'd mentioned to Brent over their many months of conversations. Reliable electricity. Never-ending fresh water. Better medical care than what her mother had gotten in the West Bank after suffering a stroke. Something as simple as being able to go into Jerusalem to buy a mini-refrigerator to keep her makeup in during heat waves, which she had found online for a price far better than on her side of the wall. She had really wanted that refrigerator, but then she factored in the cost of having to hire a taxi with special license plates to get through the checkpoints, and the humiliation of watching the Israelis inspecting the refrigerator for hidden bombs, and that was the end of that wish. But there were plenty of others. She wished she could take her nieces to the beaches on the Mediterranean. And one more thing, she was saying now—she would like not to have to wake up every week-day morning at five o'clock in order to get on the shuttle the U.S. sent into the West Bank for its employees who lived on her side of the wall, to take them to the U.S. embassy and consulate without having to go through the checkpoint. She had to pay for the shuttle, but no matter. It was better than fighting her way through the chutes, so she set her alarm for five, and then she was through the wall, and then she was back in her house every night by ten thinking the same thoughts: *I've worked hard. I'm very honest. I help a lot. I go way beyond. And I'm not going forward. I'm stuck.*

"I just want a normal life," she said. "I can live and die a hundred million times, and it won't change."

"Wait a minute," Brent said now. "You don't have to pay for the shuttle, do you?"

"I do pay for the shuttle," Tamara said. "They take it out of my paycheck."

"They make you pay? It seems—"

"I'm willing to pay. I'm willing to pay *more*," Tamara said.

They were on their way back to Jerusalem now after the meeting, passing through a stretch of desert that was either beautiful or forlorn; like everything in Israel and the West Bank, it depended on your point of view. Bedouin encampments popped up here and there along the side of the road, and they could see Israeli settlements off in the distance, filled with Jewish settlers who as far as the Palestinians were concerned were encroachers and invaders. They rode in silence as Tamara kept checking her phone, and then Brent brought up something Tamara had been telling him about earlier but had been interrupted before she could finish.

"You said it was your cousin who was shot?" he asked.

"Yes," she said. "We were under curfew, right? So what curfew means is nobody is out on the street."

"This was the Second Intifada?" Brent asked.

"No. The First. I was a teenager then," she said, talking about a period of violence in the late 1980s and early 1990s in which more than a thousand Palestinians were killed by Israelis and about two hundred Israelis were killed by Palestinians. "So he was on his home balcony. He was eating potato chips."

"How old was he?"

"Fourteen," Tamara said. "A settler stopped his car, went out, and started shooting randomly at the houses there."

"This was in Bethlehem?"

"Yeah. Near my house," Tamara said. "And one of the bullets, it was bad luck probably, because he was sitting on the balcony, and the settler started shooting, and the bullet came in his head. And he died."

"A fourteen-year-old boy?" Brent said after a moment.

"Yes. Who was killed inside his home."

They were near Jerusalem now.

"I should have bought some rice," Tamara said, remembering something she had meant to do. "I told my dad we will have salted fish for dinner. I told him, soak it in water and put it in the refrigerator, and I will prepare it when I arrive."

"Let's see," Brent said. "Tonight, I'm probably going to have frozen pizza. Or if I'm really feeling up for it, I might go for the classic chicken schnitzel and French fries."

"Mmm," Tamara said politely. She was fond of Brent. She remembered when they first met. One more naïve American, she'd thought, who believed so sweetly that honesty and hard work made a good life possible.

"Thank you so much," she said now as he pulled in to the parking lot by the wall.

"Okay," Brent said. He wished he could have driven her to her house. But he couldn't. It wasn't allowed.

"See you tomorrow," she said.

Through the wall she went, back to her house, and not long after that, Brent found himself on the balcony of a luxury apartment complex in Jerusalem, talking to a woman who was telling him about a rock that had been thrown at her.

This was Rinat.

It had happened that morning just after sunrise, she told Brent. She was driving near her house, and with no warning a rock came smashing into her windshield from the other side of the wall.

She didn't mention a Palestinian had thrown it. There was no need.

Rinat's house, which she shared with a husband and two daughters, was fifteen miles outside Jerusalem, in a neighborhood across a highway from a Palestinian village. The village was on the other side of the wall, and though she could see into the village because it was up on a hill, she had never been inside it. Instead, she turned in to an Israeli neighborhood surrounded by a high security fence, passed through a locked and monitored gate, and went home to a house that like all modern Israeli homes had a safe room in case of a rocket attack—a steel door, reinforced concrete walls, blast-resistant windows.

"The hate is so much," she said of what life as an Israeli often felt like, and if that sounded embittered, it traced back to a period when Israel had been terrorized by a wave of indiscriminate street stabbings and suicide bombings on buses and in restaurants, all carried out by Palestinians. Rinat had been in her twenties then, and the simple act of walking down a street had her waiting for the sensation at any moment of a knife going into her back, and every time she boarded a bus, she wondered if she would be getting off it alive. It was fear through and through, and years later it had hardened into a permanent expectation that the next bus was about to explode, the next stabbing was about to happen, and the next rock was about to be thrown.

So she was grateful for the wall, although she wondered sometimes what life was like on the other side of it. She had heard that in some towns, especially the smaller and more isolated ones, all of the women were required to walk behind the men. Was that true? Was it true that every woman covered, and that if they didn't cover, or if they didn't walk behind a man, they could be beaten?

She had no idea. Instead, what she did know came from rumors, and from messages on her phone posted as warnings by people on her side of the wall who were out and about.

"They are throwing rocks," one person had written one day, giving the location.

"They are throwing Molotov cocktails," another had written on the same day, with a different location.

"I don't want to live like this," Rinat said, scrolling through them, but this was life on the Jerusalem side of the wall, the version as unavailable to Tamara as Tamara's was to Rinat. In Beit Sahour this day, Tamara was home with her parents; in Jerusalem, Rinat had come with her husband and children to spend the Sabbath with her parents, and during lunch her father had told a story about a meal he'd once had with a business associate, a Palestinian, who had invited him to his Eid dinner at the end of Ramadan. "You come. No problem," he said the man had assured him, perhaps sensing his hesitation. In fact he had never been to such a dinner, and his friends told him not to go, but he felt he couldn't say no and so he followed directions to a house the man said was just off a main road, but which turned out to be way, way off the road in an isolated neighborhood where there were no Jews whatsoever. Should he have been nervous? Maybe, but he wasn't, even when the meal was served and everyone started reaching into the piles of food and eating with their hands. *Really? Hands?* he'd thought. *No utensils? No plates?* But it was fine, he said, he enjoyed himself, he was glad he had done it once in his life, though he wouldn't again.

It was a good story, well told, and everyone had laughed at the end, including Brent, who was there because he had become friends with Rinat's brother, who had invited him. After lunch was over and the dishes were cleared, Brent went out on the balcony. It was eleven floors up with a spectacular view of Jerusalem, and Brent was looking to the southeast, in the direction of Bethlehem and, just beyond, Beit Sahour, when Rinat mentioned that she used to go to those places as a child.

That was in the early 1980s, and then came the First Intifada.

That was followed by the Second Intifada in the early 2000s, in which nearly five thousand Palestinians and more than a thousand Israelis were killed.

Then came the wall.

And now Rinat was telling Brent about the rock that smashed into her windshield, and the hatred aimed at her because she was an Israeli and a Jew, and that she had no idea what would happen if she ever tried to go to the other side of the wall, but that it didn't matter because in all likelihood she never would.

ANOTHER SATURDAY, and there were rumors going around that Hamas was planning some kind of attack with long-range rockets that were aimed at Tel Aviv and perhaps Jerusalem too. As a result, Jerusalem, always quiet on the Sabbath, felt quieter than usual, and Brent was inside his apartment, catching up on the news from America, where there had been a Trump rally in Georgia a hundred or so miles from his home.

"Lock her up!" the crowd chanted at one point, after Trump had referred to Hillary Clinton as "crooked Hillary," and as they kept chanting, Trump had waved his hands like a conductor, urging them on. "You're great people. You're great people," he had told them, and Brent wondered: Did Trump understand what he was encouraging? Did he understand the violence it could lead to? And what about the people chanting? Did they have any understanding of violence? Not wrestling-match violence, but true violence, the kind that changes the soul not only of a person but of a country?

The longer Brent stayed in Israel, the more he wondered about Trump's motives. Without a doubt, some Americans did understand violence, especially ones who had long been marginalized and discriminated against, but what about the vast majority of Americans? What about the Trump supporters who at rallies laughed at Trump's bullying, cheered his taunts, fist-pumped his insults, and reacted so primally to his incitements?

"I'd like to punch him in the face," Trump had said at a rally about a protester, to roars.

"Knock the crap out of them," he urged the crowd at another rally, to more roars.

"You people were vicious, violent, screaming, 'Where's the wall? We want the wall!' Screaming, 'Prison! Prison! Lock her up!'" he'd said to his supporters after he'd won the election. "I mean, you are going crazy. I mean you were nasty and mean and vicious . . ."

In Iraq once, some of Brent's soldiers had shot a child by mistake. It was on a day when roadside bombs were going off everywhere, the soldiers were laying down suppressive fire after two of those explosions rocked their Humvees, and one of the rounds went through a living room window and into the head of an unlucky girl who in another place, another time, another war, would be a boy on a balcony eating a potato chip.

So those soldiers knew violence, as did the soldiers

who discovered the body of an Iraqi who had been secretly helping them. He had been killed by having his
head squeezed in a vise, and that was how the soldiers
had found him, still in the vise, left there deliberately not
as a sign of what could happen to one person but to make
everyone else—everyone not in the vise—fear it could
happen to them.

That was violence, too.

The act—and then the reaction to the act. There were
so many layers to violence, which Brent was learning
anew in Jerusalem, and had learned again and again in
Iraq, including the moral reckonings afterward, which
eventually became corrosive and often ended up in
dreams. Look at what had happened to Aieti, the soldier
who had once said "If there's a pill that would stop
dreams, I'd take it right now." He'd been talking about
his own dream of the day a Humvee he was in drove over
a buried bomb. His leg had been broken in the explosion,
yet he'd managed to pull two bleeding soldiers to safety
as the Humvee burst into flames, but what he would
dream of was the driver no one could get to, who in the
dream would show up on fire, always on fire and asking
Aieti, "Why didn't you save me?"

The poor driver, who was only nineteen. And poor
Aieti, who wanted so badly to dream of anything else.
And what about Prestley, the soldier who on especially
bad days would say to Brent, "Fuck it, sir. Let's go eat."
What had been his dreams? Away he'd gone from the
war, home to a wife and two young daughters and a house
in the Kansas countryside, where a few years later fire-
fighters responded to a call about a fire. By the time they

arrived, the flames were sky-high. They found Prestley out front, slumped in the driver's seat of his car, dead from a shotgun blast fired into the right side of his head. Then, inside the house, they found his wife and his five-year-old daughter, both of whom had been shot, too. They were all dead, and it didn't take long to figure out what had happened. Prestley had done it all. He had shot his wife, and his daughter, and then had set his house on fire and killed himself, and the only survivor in the family was his other daughter, who was in school when they called her out of class, and then was on her way to the police station dialing her mother's cell phone, and when her mother didn't answer, her father's, and when he didn't answer, her mother's again, and then her father's again, and then was moving into the rest of her life where she'd find herself thinking sometimes about the days she knew her father was taking his antidepressants because he would open the curtains, and sometimes about what had happened a few days before he did what he did, when they were all in the car and he began bashing his head against the passenger window and saying, "We're going to be fine, we're going to be fine, God will save us, I'm sorry, I'm sorry."

Sitting in his apartment, Brent wanted more than anything for it to be Monday, so he would be busy again and not be thinking about such things. He hated Saturdays because now, in the quiet, his thoughts were moving on to all of the soldiers and the way they would come in from missions sometimes and just want to talk.

"Hey, sir, what are we doing this for?" one asked one time, and Brent assured him that it was okay to ask, it was okay to be concerned, it was okay even to be scared, and that what they were doing had purpose and meaning.

To which the soldier said, "I can't sleep, sir. I can't sleep. Do you sleep, sir?"

So that soldier knew one of the most damning truths of violence, the warping effect of it, as did all of the soldiers, as did the Iraqis, as did the Israelis, as did the Palestinians, as did Rinat, as did Tamara, and as did Brent himself because he was still judging himself on what had happened at the end of the deployment, when he had begun chanting, "Die, monkey, die." That moment, that phrase, was who he had become in Iraq, after starting out with so much hope. He had become furious, and now, all these years later, that fury had turned into a feeling of shame as he sat in his apartment, checking his work phone for any updates about the rumored rocket attack.

Nothing.

He picked up his other phone, his personal one, and began looking at videos from home, little clips recorded by the camera in the doorbell Laura had bought.

"This is Laura bringing the dog in at twilight."

"Here's Laura putting bug spray on Meredith."

"Her little backpack on," he said, looking at another of Meredith, walking out to the school bus with Laura. He looked closer. "Actually it's a big backpack. Like she's hiking the Himalayas. Like she's a Sherpa."

He was laughing. He was a little teary. He called Laura, who put Meredith on the line.

"Hi, Mer."

She whispered something he couldn't hear.

"What?"

She said it again, louder.

"I want you to come home," she said.

ANOTHER SATURDAY NOW, his final one.

"Thirty minutes," his taxi driver said when they arrived at the airport, looking at his watch, surprised at
how quick the trip had been, even on a Sabbath. "I wasn't
even trying to drive fast."

"Huh?" Brent said.

He was once again lost in thought. He was about to
get on a plane. He was about to retire from the Army, go
home to America, become a civilian, and see up close
what the country he had spent twenty-eight years defending was turning into.

"Thirty minutes," the driver repeated.

"Yeah?" Brent said, and soon he was on his way home
to a country with a president who was tweeting about
"Sleepy Joe" and "Crooked Hillary" and "the Lamestream
Media" and "DEMOCRAT WITCH HUNT!" That was
what Trump was thinking, and Brent was thinking: *Here
I come.*

CHAPTER 6

LAURA HAD GOTTEN Brent a welcome-home gift, a lawn sign that had been installed the night before while he was flying toward America and she was sitting alone outside on the front steps listening to the sounds of a summer evening in Pleasantville. The crickets. The tree frogs and katydids. A plane buzzing somewhere high overhead in a sky so humid the stars seemed smudged, and a slow-moving car rolling up the street and turning in to the driveway next door. It was Michael, coming home in his van. "Hi, Laura," she heard him call. "How are you?" she called back. "Tired," he said. She listened in the darkness to the grinding sound of the wheelchair ramp lowering and raising, the whir of the van's doors opening and closing, and then the garage door opening and closing as Michael wheeled himself into his house. "It takes so *long*," she had said quietly, talking to herself, marveling at what it must be like to be Michael all the time, and then she heard another car coming, which pulled up in front of the house. A worker from a business called Card My Yard got out and began constructing a sign on the front lawn letter by letter, each letter on a metal pole pushed into the soft grass. "Enjoy!" the woman had said to Laura when she had finished, and that was the sign Brent had seen when he arrived home and that Laura walked by now in the late afternoon, out for a walk with the dog.

THE COLONEL IS IN THE HOUSE, it read.

She paused to look at it.

"He *is* in the house," she said to the dog.

By the time she got back, Brent was sound asleep, and when he woke before sunup, she was the one asleep, so he went to Waffle House on his own and ordered the All-Star Special with bacon *and* sausage.

"All the way on the pork products," he said, having said no such thing in the past year in Jerusalem.

He went to the grocery store, where they were frying chicken in the deli.

"The smell of America," he said.

He was, in these first hours home, loving everything about his country. Whatever he had been feeling in Israel was gone, even the chagrin he'd felt just before leaving when he had read about an altercation in a grocery store only a few miles from where he was now, which had begun when a man who wasn't black had approached a woman who was black in the express line. The man had pointed to the ten-item-limit sign, the woman had pointed at him, and off it went. Words were exchanged. The police were called. The woman said the man told her, "You need to go back where you came from." The man said he had called her a "lazy bitch" and nothing more. Witnesses emerged with conflicting accounts. A surveillance video was released and scrutinized as if it were the Zapruder film of the Kennedy assassination. Social media posts were liked and shared and retweeted and got millions of views, and very quickly people on the left were saying the man was the latest echo of Trump's hateful rhetoric and people on the right were saying the woman was one more example of liberalism run amok and some people were saying the woman was standing up for the rights of victimized women everywhere and other people were saying it was all the media's fault, and on it had spiraled and was still spiraling.

But not here. Here, the air smelled of freshly fried chicken. And the worker bagging the groceries, unlike the sourpuss workers in Jerusalem, said "May I help you?" And the waitress at Waffle House had called him "Honey." And the car dealership he took his pickup truck to for an oil change had a free coffee bar and massage chairs. "We're here to WOW ya!" was the dealership's slogan, and it was 135,000 square feet of gleaming American wow, all due to what its website called the "roll up your sleeves and get it done" attitude of its owners, a man named Mike, who at age twelve "began working 7 days a week and never slowed down," and his wife, Linda, a "farmer's daughter" with bright blond hair, bright white teeth, and a bright gold cross on her necklace who "was born and raised in Oklahoma, where she was equally at home in a beauty pageant or 4-H competition."

Was there any other country he could love so much? Even the weather delighted him. "This thunderstorm is perfect," he said at the end of his second full day home, sitting on his front porch.

HIS ONE WORRY was about life after the Army, a day that was getting ever closer.

"I've always wondered: What do civilians do? What does a businessman do?" he had said once when he was still in Jerusalem and starting to think seriously about life after the Army. He'd just heard from a friend in Atlanta about a job working with veterans and was going to apply for it, but he had no idea how to go about that and called Laura for help.

"Desired salary," he'd said, reading the application to her. "Should I put my colonel pay here?"

"No, they're not going to pay you that much. They're a nonprofit," she'd said. She was busy trying to get grading finished for the college courses she taught so she could go see her mother so she could be home in time for Meredith's bus, but she took a moment to do a quick online search for how much a job like that might pay. "I guess you could put eighty thousand."

"I'll just put, fuck, I don't know, a hundred ten thousand."

"No, don't put that."

"Why not?"

"Okay. Just put it. Just apply. Whatever."

"And then do you think I should do a cover letter?"

"It's up to you. I don't think anybody looks at cover letters anymore."

"That's what I thought."

"Just, whatever."

So he didn't get that job, and now, home, on the way in the predawn darkness to Waffle House, he'd seen cars already lined up to turn south on the highway to downtown Atlanta. Civilian cars. Businessman cars. The highway itself was nothing but brake lights—an hour minimum to go thirty miles—and for what? A cubicle in an office tower, like the one with the Coca-Cola logo on top, where the entire purpose of everyone in that building was to sell one more case, one more can, one more ounce of Coca-Cola than the day before? Did a life such as that life have meaning?

He tried to imagine other options, such as teaching. His mother had been a teacher. His sister was a teacher. Maybe he could do that, but then he imagined his first day in front of students.

"Good morning, class. I don't like loud, sudden noises."

So maybe not teaching.

For a while, he had been interested in politics. To be a senator, or a representative, had seemed to him the highest form of civilian service other than being president, so much so that before he went to Jerusalem, he'd signed up for a two-day seminar on how to run for office. It had been put on in Washington, D.C., by an organization trying to get more military vets in Congress, and Brent was serious enough about it, and dreamy enough, to spring for a thousand dollars on plane fare and a hotel, and to pack a blue blazer and a dry-cleaned shirt.

Day One:

There were thirty people in all, and every man was in

a blue blazer except for two who were so eager they had gone full suit. He was off to a good start.

The first speaker told them they would need to knock on fifty to a hundred doors a day, every day, from March through Election Day and that there was door-knocking software they could purchase to help them keep track. That was for local office, he said, and if they were going to run for Congress, forget door-knocking. They would need five million dollars minimum, unless they were running to represent a rural district, which might only be two million.

The second speaker talked about the need for clear, concise, consistent, and compelling communication skills, and Brent noticed that some people were writing down all of those c-words on legal pads in leather folders. He grabbed a blank sheet of paper and began writing, too.

Next came an exercise. Everyone lined up in two rows and had a few seconds to introduce themselves as a pretend candidate to the person across from them.

"Hi, I'm Brent Cummings," he said, following instructions. He stood straight. No hands in pockets. Eyeball-to-eyeball contact. "I'm here at the workshop just trying to figure out if this is even something I want to do, or I can do, and that's what I'm trying to get answers to, to learn about running. I have a passion for politics, but is it even feasible to do after I leave the Army?"

He tried again, this time with instructions to focus on an issue he was passionate about.

"Hey, how ya doing? My name's Brent Cummings," he said. "I'm passionate about conservation, and I just wanted to talk to you about what I feel is important, to keep lands that we cherish in this nation, and the value that we have from those lands that we've had from the past, to be able to share it with our children in the future. To me, what that means is open access. Being able to share it and not lose it. If we don't protect those lands, we'll lose them. So that's what I'm after, and I'd like to, you know, encourage your support."

He'd neglected to mention he was running for office. Another try.

"Hey, Greg, how ya doing? My name's Brent Cummings, I'm passionate about conservation, I just wanted to talk to you about it for a moment."

"I *love* conservation," Greg said.

"Great. Well, to me what conservation means is the ability to protect and look after lands that we have and that make us unique and different than the other countries in this world—our national parks, our open lands— and I want to be able to preserve that for the future, just like it's been preserved for us in the past," he said. "And . . ."

Blah blah blah.

Now he listened to Greg's pitch.

"I'm running for a random seat in the House in Massachusetts, and let me tell you the reason why I'm running. I'm running because I think every person, every family, in our community should have the same access to the quality of health care that I had when I was in active duty service. And I can tell you firsthand the reason I'm passionate about this is because I was a health care provider when I was active duty, I work with veterans in the

VA now, and it's the foundation of a healthy society, a healthy people, people who can reach their fullest potential, and I want every one of us to reach our potential."

They shook hands. Brent laughed. He looked like he was ready to vote for Greg.

There were more speakers, and they droned on through the afternoon, with all kinds of advice. You'll need to do opposition research not only on your opponent, but also on yourself. Don't expect people to vote for you just because you were in the military. Do expect to raise a minimum of $10,000 a day. Treat every day as a day to raise money. There's never a day off from that. Don't be shy about asking the people you love for donations, and if you can't do that, forget about it.

"This is a blood sport."

"Most of you aren't going to win."

"Are you being Don Quixote and going after something that's not winnable, or is there something there?"

That night, Brent looked over some of the handouts he'd been given.

One was a list of "Personal Questions." "Ever done drugs?" "Any affairs?" "Any family members have run-ins with the law?" "Are you willing to release your taxes?" "Willing to release your school transcripts?" "Ever miss a payment on your car / mortgage / credit cards?"

Another was a list of "Killer Questions" any candidate should know the answers to. "Price of a gallon of milk?" "Favorite place to eat when in district?" "Minimum wage rate in district?" "How many women / African American / gay / Latino staffers do you have?" "Last book you read?" "Last movie you saw?"

He kept looking. Where were the parts about meaning and purpose?

Day Two:

"Well, I'm not running for office," he said.

So no senator. No representative. No teacher. No working with veterans. What was left?

It was at times like this he missed his father, who would know just what to say.

There were other men he had looked up to as well, not to the extent of his father but enough that he missed their advice too. One was his old high school football coach, a man named John Bauer, who would say some of the weirdest things Brent had ever heard. "Ivory soap is one hundred percent pure and it floats—and so does shit," he would say to the team, his version of inspiration. "You block like I screw—slow and sloppy." "You couldn't get laid if you had fifty fifty-dollar bills in your hand in a whorehouse." "Your ass sucks boxcars" was one of his most inscrutable, along with what he said one day to a teammate of Brent's: "You're like a BB in a boxcar." "What does that mean?" he'd asked. Brent had no idea—none of them did—and yet something about Bauer had been so inspiring that he coached his team to forty-six straight victories, and when he died years later, it was the first time Brent had experienced the death of someone he loved. The day it happened, Brent had been coming home from college for Thanksgiving break, and when he got into the car with his father, just the two of them, a chance to talk about things and get some advice, his father told him he had been fired that morning from his job. Not that he had quit, but that he had been fired.

So two men became mortal that day.

There was a third man Brent looked up to, still alive but old now, and Brent decided to go see him. His name was Chick Chafin, and Brent had met him early in his Army career, when they happened to meet one Sunday at church.

As Brent would learn about Chick over the decades to come, he spoke plainly. Both of his children had been born with microcephaly, a birth defect in which a baby's head is smaller than normal. The older of the two children was sixty-one now, the younger was fifty-eight, and Chick was eighty-seven and nearing the end of a life that in many ways was a mirror of Brent's. He, too, had been an Army infantry officer in war. In his case, it had been Vietnam. He, too, had come home with memories of things he had done, or as he described it, "I still dream about some of that crap." Brent hit it off with him immediately, and when Meredith was born, the way Chick regarded his children, and treated them, turned out to be far more helpful than what the church ladies kept saying:

"You must be very special for God to choose you to have this child."

Brent wanted to strangle them.

And then there was Chick.

"You know, both of my kids are retarded," he said one day, not long after Meredith had been born.

The word surprised Brent. He had been taught to never say such a thing. Instead of protesting, though, he kept listening.

"You have a blessing, but you also have responsibilities," Chick went on. He didn't say a lot more than that, but Brent learned what he meant by watching him. His son, Jeff, needed a shot every day, and except for the times he had been deployed, Chick had been giving him his shot for fifty-six years. His wife, Barbara, needed four shots a day for diabetes, and every day he gave her four shots. His daughter, Susan, could be prickly at times, and he never lost his temper. Jeff got a job at a barbecue restaurant, and for twenty-four years Chick drove him there and picked him up, and when they sat sometimes and had lunch, and the iced tea came in a big glass, and Jeff said, "I want the small glass," Chick would explain, patiently, always patiently, "Just because it's a big glass doesn't mean you have to drink it all."

The last time Brent had seen Chick was before Jerusalem, and it had shocked him to see this man who had always seemed so sturdy to him leaning on a cane. Now, two years later, he looked significantly older, and he told Brent the time had come for his family, all of them, to move into adjoining rooms at an assisted living facility, where they would remain for the rest of their lives.

Am I going to see this man again? Brent wondered.

"I have something I want to give you," Chick said, maybe thinking the same thing. It was a shotgun, one Chick had used whenever they'd gone quail hunting.

"You don't have to," Brent said. "I don't deserve—"

"Yes, you do, and you're going to take it," Chick said.

"Yes, sir," Brent said.

One of the things Chick had taught him, again by example, was to say what was on his mind, so he did.

"I love you, Chick," he said.

"My hunting days are over," Chick said, and the honesty of it stayed with Brent as he headed home, along with something Chick's son had said when they were saying goodbye.

"I don't know what will happen," he'd said. "My dad will die, and who will take care of me?"

Who was going to take care of Meredith? That was how Brent had heard it, and it was on his mind more and more as he looked at job websites, sent out résumés, heard nothing back. Why couldn't he find anything? And why did everyone keep asking him about it?

"You got a job yet?" the service adviser at the car dealership had asked when he mentioned he was getting out of the Army after twenty-eight years.

An old friend called.

"Well, tell me about what's next for Brent Cummings," he said.

"Well, I'm working on a couple of things," Brent said.

Another old friend called.

"What are you going to do for a job to pay for that big-ass fucking house?"

He got an email out of the blue from his old high school friend Irene, that laughing girl he would send flying into the roof of his old VW every time he flew over a bump. "Thank you Brent for all your sacrifices," she wrote. "Thank you," he wrote back, but what he wanted to write was, "What does it fucking matter, Irene?"

"He doesn't feel like he has any purpose right now," Laura said one day, after the biggest fight they'd had since they got married. At one point, Brent got so frustrated he picked up something from a table and threw it, and though it wasn't aimed at anyone, that was something he'd never done. She was still hearing what he'd said before he had driven off, that if he died that day, he'd be worth more than he would once he retired.

A few days later, a hundred or so people gathered for his retirement ceremony.

"This is your day!" his mother said, hugging him tightly.

"Well," Brent said, not telling her, or anyone, that he had awakened at two-thirty and stayed awake for a few hours trying to fight off his dream.

A friend asked, "So, you going to give a speech or something?"

"Yeah, I got some things to say," Brent said, and then the ceremony started and he was in tears. "Bear with me as this old soldier now chokes up a bit and says thanks," he told everyone.

There was a lot of clapping that day, including when the person overseeing the ceremony announced, "At this time, Brent will receive a certificate of appreciation from the president of the United States." As it happened, Trump on that day was in the midst of his first impeachment trial, but in this place, filled with people who had voted for him, the clapping continued as Brent gave the certificate a quick look. "My best wishes to you for happiness and success in the future," it read in part. "Donald J. Trump, Commander in Chief."

He didn't cry then, not when he saw that signature, but he did when he was given an American flag "for his faithful service to the nation," and again when he thanked Laura, Emily, Meredith, his mother and his long-gone father—"I miss you, Dad," he said—and then again when he tried for a moment to talk about that very first death in Iraq.

"Jay died at a place called Mashtal, at a little intersection," he said, and couldn't finish the sentence.

More clapping, more tears, and that was that. He was a civilian now.

ON BRENT'S FIRST DAY as a civilian, Donald Trump tweeted, "Trump poll numbers are the highest since election, despite constant phony Witch Hunts! Tens of thousands of people attending rallies (which the Fake News never mentions) to see 'The Greatest Show On Earth'. Fun because USA is WINNING AGAIN!"

On Brent's second day as a civilian, Trump tweeted, "The Radical Left, Do Nothing Democrats, don't want justice when pushing the Impeachment Hoax, they only want to destabilize the Republican Party so they can do better in the 2020 election, & that includes the House & Senate. They are playing with the people by taking it this far!"

On Brent's third day as a civilian, Trump tweeted, "I hope Republicans & the American people realize that the totally partisan Impeachment Hoax is exactly that, a Hoax."

On Brent's fourth day as a civilian, Trump delivered his State of the Union address and said, "I am thrilled to report to you tonight that our economy is the best it has ever been. Our military is completely rebuilt, with its power being unmatched anywhere in the world, and it's not even close. Our borders are secure. Our families are

flourishing. Our values are renewed. Our pride is re-
stored. And for all of these reasons, I say to the people of
our great country and to the Members of Congress: The
state of our Union is stronger than ever before."

On Brent's fifth day as a civilian, Trump tweeted, "I
will be making a public statement tomorrow at 12:00pm
from the @WhiteHouse to discuss our Country's VIC-
TORY on the Impeachment Hoax!"

On Brent's sixth day as a civilian, Trump delivered a
nationwide address in which he said, "We've been going
through this now for over three years. It was evil. It was
corrupt. It was dirty cops. It was leakers and liars. And
this should never, ever happen to another president—
ever. I don't know that other presidents would have been
able to take it. Some people said, no, they wouldn't have.
But I can tell you, at a minimum, you have to focus on
this because it can get away very quickly. No matter who
you have with you, it can get away very quickly. It was a
disgrace."

On Brent's seventh day as a civilian, Trump tweeted,
"Just had a long and very good conversation by phone
with President Xi of China. He is strong, sharp and pow-
erfully focused on leading the counterattack on the Coro-
navirus. He feels they are doing very well, even building
hospitals in a matter of only days. Nothing is easy,
but . . ."

". . . . he will be successful, especially as the weather
starts to warm & the virus hopefully becomes weaker,
and then gone. Great discipline is taking place in China,
as President Xi strongly leads what will be a very successful operation. We are working closely with China to help!"

On Brent's eighth day as a civilian, Trump tweeted, "Crazy Nancy Pelosi's Impeachment Hoax has lifted Republican Congressional Polls (she lost the House once before!), and my Polls, WAY UP, which was expected, but it has had a great effect on Republican Senate races, including North Carolina, Kentucky, Colorado and Arizona. Thanks!"

On Brent's ninth day as a civilian, Trump tweeted, "FBI Director Christopher Wray just admitted that the FISA Warrants and Survailence [sic] of my campaign were illegal. So was the Fake Dossier. THEREFORE, THE WHOLE SCAM INVESTIGATION, THE MUELLER REPORT AND EVERYTHING ELSE FOR THREE YEARS, WAS A FIXED HOAX. WHO PAYS THE PRICE?...."

".... This is the biggest political crime in American History, by far. SIMPLY PUT, THE PARTY IN POWER ILLEGALLY SPIED ON MY CAMPAIGN, BOTH BEFORE AND AFTER THE ELECTION, IN ORDER TO CHANGE OR NULLIFY THE RESULTS OF THE ELECTION. IT CONTINUED ON WITH THE IMPEACHMENT HOAX. Terrible!"

"DRAIN THE SWAMP!"

"MAKE AMERICA GREAT AGAIN and then, KEEP AMERICA GREAT!"

On Brent's tenth day as a civilian, he got a job.

HE GOT IT the way some people might say the system works for other people, and what those other people might say is how the system works when you roll up your sleeves and get it done. What Brent would say is it traced back all the way to January 2007, when he was a few weeks away from going to Iraq.

He was in Kansas then, at Fort Riley, which had so many birds flying above its one hundred thousand acres that one of those TV hunting shows came to film an episode about quail hunting. Brent, who loved hunting at Fort Riley, was invited to watch. He showed up with his dog Tucker, and when one of the hunters said, "Hey, boy, I hear they got some prairie chickens out there," Brent said, "Yeah, they got some prairie chickens." Brent didn't yet know who the man was, that he had once been one of the most connected people in Washington, D.C., described in a book as "a southern, tough-talking, Jack Daniels–drinking, boyishly handsome, charismatic lawyer who long ago made the right connections on his way up north . . ." He just knew the man's name was Jim and he wanted to hunt, and while the hunters who would be on the TV show went one way, the two of them and Tucker went the other, got some birds, and shared a great afternoon. "You keep your head down and stay in touch," Jim said, and Brent did just that.

Jim, it turned out, was the head of an organization called the Theodore Roosevelt Conservation Partnership, or TRCP. In Iraq, Brent added him to his email distribution list, and when he came home, Jim invited him to hunt on his ranch in Montana.

And that was how Brent met a man named Weldon, who was also involved in the Theodore Roosevelt Conservation Partnership and was there to hunt too.

They went hunting, and afterward Weldon introduced

Brent to a man named Sandy, owner of an exclusive hunting and shooting club, and that was how Brent became an honorary member of a club with a long waiting list that cost thousands of dollars to join.

Weldon also began inviting Brent to TRCP's annual dinner, and that was where, just before he left for Jerusalem, he met Sandy's son-in-law Todd, who said that when Brent came home, they should have breakfast.

So they had breakfast, and Todd said Brent should meet his business partner, Tom.

Who said that Brent should meet a friend of his, also named Tom, who owned one of the largest construction companies in Atlanta.

They met in the boardroom. It was more formal than friendly. It lasted an hour, and Brent left thinking he'd exhausted that string, but then Tom texted him to say he would set up a meeting between Brent and his friend Ken, who was the chief of police in a town called Sandy Springs just north of Atlanta.

"Why would I meet with the Sandy Springs police chief?" Brent thought.

"Why are you meeting the Sandy Springs police chief?" Laura asked when he told her where he was going.

"I don't know. Whatever," Brent said, but he went, and he made a good impression on Ken, just as he had on Tom, and Tom, and Todd, and Sandy, and Weldon, and Jim, and when Brent mentioned he was just back from Israel, Ken mentioned he was on the board of an organization that helped train police officers to become better officers by sending them on exchange trips to Israel, and it just so happened the organization was looking for someone to help run it.

And that was how thirteen years after quail hunting in Kansas, and ten days after becoming a civilian, Brent got a job. Even though he'd be joining the line of brake lights to downtown Atlanta, it didn't feel like a Coca-Cola job. Especially at first, before he was maligned as a white male Israeli-loving Palestinian-hating racist, it felt as though his promised American life was still on track.

CHAPTER 7

ELEVEN WEEKS LATER, Brent's concern was no longer about the dreadful commute. It was about whether he would ever go anywhere again. He was home. Everyone was home. Everything was shut down, and it seemed like forever since the day Trump had sent out that tweet about President Xi and the virus, ". . . he will be successful, especially as the weather starts to warm & the virus hopefully becomes weaker, and then gone."

The virus wasn't gone.

It wasn't weaker.

Xi hadn't been successful.

The only part in that entire tweet that had come true was the part about the weather. It was warm enough now for bees to be out, and Brent was on his porch trying to find one.

It was a big, plump, slow-moving carpenter bee. He'd seen it go into a hole at the base of his porch railing and it hadn't come out, so it was in there, somewhere. He got down on his knees, and then his stomach, wiggled forward with a stick, and pushed the stick into the hole as far as it would go.

The bee began making a sound, like a high-pitched whine.

"It's a bee! You can hear it!" Laura said, coming out to see what Brent was up to now.

"That little fucker," Brent said.

"Get a coat hanger," Laura suggested, and she went inside and came back out with one, which Brent straightened and pushed into the hole.

The whining got louder. Brent pushed the hanger in as far as it could go, but still the whining continued. This was some bee.

Laura went back into the house and came out with a new type of wasp-and-hornet spray she'd gotten, one that shot out foam.

"Well, that's not going to work," Brent said.

"Well, just try it," Laura said, so he aimed the nozzle at the hole and was in the midst of spraying when he heard Michael.

"Hey, Colonel!"

"Hey, neighbor," he called back, still on his stomach, "I'm trying to get this carpenter bee," and then he stood up because he hadn't talked to Michael much at all since he'd been home.

He leaned against the porch railing. He had his new puppy with him, another black Lab to replace Tucker, this one named Finn, and Michael had his dog Scout, a small, furry, eleven-year-old mix. They talked about dogs for a bit, and at some point, Michael said, "I'm glad our governor's getting things reopened."

"Yeah, I'm just frustrated at the national level," Brent said.

"What do you mean?" Michael asked.

And that was when, for the first time in all of their conversations over the years, Brent decided to say something about Trump.

Before his retirement, he never would have done such a thing. He had been taught over and over that soldiers weren't supposed to voice public opinions about their commander in chief, not unless there was something going on that was illegal, unethical, or immoral. That was the standard. It wasn't blind loyalty, but necessary respectfulness. Soldiers follow orders, after all. But since retiring, he had slowly begun to speak out loud about things, getting used to the idea of free expression, or at least freer expression, and now, referring to what Trump had been saying about the growing pandemic, he said to Michael, "He really lost me when he said, 'I take no responsibility.'"

"What do you mean?" Michael asked again, maybe a little sharper, and for the next half hour, things took off from there, leaving everyone with their own differing memories of what happened.

Laura, for instance, would remember going inside to do a puzzle and thinking, "Shut up. Stop talking."

Michael would remember saying to Brent, "Colonel, let's understand each other about something. I hate everything liberal," and Brent replying, "I hear you."

"I want this to be clear. I am a Trump supporter. I am a hard-core conservative and far right. I believe in the Bible and the U.S. Constitution—as they were written."

"I understand."

And Brent would remember saying to Michael:

"I was very disappointed in the president, but not surprised because he's not a good leader. A leader takes full responsibility."

And then went further:

"He lies. He lies to us every day."

"When has he ever done that?" Michael asked.

So Brent started listing the lies.

"Well, all politicians lie."

"But all politicians don't lie all the time. And that's what he does. He lies all the time," Brent said and listed more examples.

"I hadn't heard that," Michael said. "I haven't seen that. I haven't seen any of that."

Brent began mentioning sources, and Michael pushed back, saying those sources were the liars, not Trump, that the mainstream media lied all the time, incessantly and deliberately, and the proof was that they never, never went after the left, only the right.

"Yeah, yeah, I understand that point," Brent said, but the larger point was that leaders should be held to the highest of standards, and Trump was violating that standard every day.

"I don't trust the man," Brent said. "I don't trust him with your life, with my life, with any life on this street."

And then added, "He's un-Christian."

At least that's the way he would remember the conversation, along with a growing sense that things were getting heated and that if they kept going, they were going to cross a line that would be difficult to cross back. He tried to bring things to a cooler level.

"I'm just frustrated," he said. "I do want to rally around our flag. I do want to support our president."

"Hey, Colonel, I respect you," Michael said.

"Well, I really enjoyed talking," Brent said. "Gotta get back to the bees."

He liked Michael. He admired him, and he liked having him as his neighbor. But this, now, felt different. Until that conversation, Brent hadn't realized how devoted Michael was to Trump, and he couldn't help but wonder whether that devotion would be returned. What would Trump think of Michael? What if Michael were invited to the Oval Office and he went in not walking but wheeling himself in his chair? Would Trump take Michael's imperfect hand and shake it? Would he mock him afterward like he had mocked other people? He fell from a tree? Winners don't fall from trees. Losers fall from trees.

It was easier for Brent to imagine what Trump would think of him.

"I'm the ideal. White, guy, veteran. I would fit the American dream for him."

"I THINK HE would like me," Michael was saying of Trump. "I don't see any reason why he wouldn't. I think he would find me to be a good American."

He'd been up since two-thirty, as usual, and sunup was still an hour away when he pulled in to a parking lot at a park near his house. Leg unstrapped, doors open, ramp down. His fingers on his left hand were taped together to help him roll his chair. From the beginning, he was dead set on being in a chair that he would power himself, rather than relying on a battery, and he had worked painfully hard to make that happen, velcroing his fingers to a dowel and rolling the dowel back and forth, over and over, trying to get his fingers to curl and uncurl. That had taken a while, but now it was his fingers and hands working the wheels, along with whatever upper body strength he had from lifting weights and going for long rolls before work.

The parking lot was empty. There was a paved handicapped spot, which was helpful, but the lot itself was covered with uneven gravel that was difficult to roll across. As maddening as that might have been, he did it without complaint. Then he had to navigate a two-lane road for fifty yards that was slick from overnight rain, and when a car came around a curve on a direct line for Michael, the driver hit his brakes and skidded. The car eased past. Michael kept rolling. Then came a sidewalk that looked level to the naked eye but actually pitched to the right, making his roll that much harder, and a boardwalk with rotting boards here and there, the locations of which he had memorized from previous trips because if a wheel hit a hole, and the chair tipped, and he fell, then what?

It was all so perilous, that was the thing. When he was first injured, his doctor said someone with his version of quadriplegia could expect to live another thirty years with a good diet and exercise, and he had just passed the twenty-eight-year mark. His goal this morning was five and a half miles in ninety minutes, including stops for Scout, who trotted alongside him on a leash. "Come on, Scout. You know the drill," he said, and began rolling faster, glad for the things he still could feel as a C7 quad, including his expanding lungs and accelerating heart.

"Thank you, Lord," he said as he rolled. Sometimes he said the words out loud, usually he said them to himself. He wasn't overly religious, but this was something he liked to do. It was quiet except for a million frogs. It was breezeless but it wasn't yet hot. He liked the smell of the trees, even the type of pine tree from which he had fallen. "I am thinking through things with the Lord," he said. Almost a mile done now, and he prayed for his health to continue and, on the day it didn't, a heaven of sound bodies and no wheelchairs. He prayed for Ann, and for his daughter who he didn't think he'd see ever again, and for the country, and for all of the people who didn't thank God for Trump, as he was thanking God now.

Three years before, it would have been different. His vote in 2016 had been an anti-Hillary vote, pure and simple. "I was very nervous about Donald Trump whenever he first came down the escalator in 2015," was his explanation about that. "I thought to myself: Is this a gentleman?"

But gradually, he said, he came to realize that Trump was the first politician in his entire life he could feel speaking directly to him—or as he described it: "Well, I did a little bit of research about the guy. I looked at what he was saying, what the Dems were trying to do to America, and then I read his book, well, I listened to it on audiotape, about making America great again. I got it from the public library up there off Post Road, and I listened to it on the way to work, and I understood what he was talking about. This country is based on freedom, our rights, capitalist society, you do your absolute best, the best you possibly can do to make a living. You should not *depend* on government. We pay our taxes for clean water, clean air, the police, security, programs to help people that need it. We do *not* pay taxes to have the government take care of us. And the way I saw it coming was that today's leftist, Democratic party—there are no more moderate Democrats, they're gone—today's leftist party wants the government to take over and dictate to the citizenry their health care, their housing, that's what the government on the left today wants . . ."

One thing Michael could talk about with the same level of enthusiasm he had for Trump was his disdain for the Democratic Party.

". . . and Donald Trump is against all that. Today's leftist, Marxist, communistic Democrat Party, they openly tell you socialism is what they want. Socialism has failed every time in the world. Donald Trump has stood up and said we will never be a socialist country, while Sanders and AOC and the Squad sit over there smirking like 'Wait until we get rid of you.' It makes me so scared that they're trying to do this to the United States when that is not what this country was founded upon. In the seventeen hundreds, we had to fight for our freedom from the British. They were a tyrannical government. They wanted to take our guns, they wanted to take our speech, they wanted to take everything and do what they wanted to do with this great continent of ours we call America.

Today's Democrats? They are a tyrannical government wanting to do the same thing that we fought for back then—the first time I have ever seen this in my fifty-six years of living. And I'm not educated on politics, I just know what I see as an American man. I just, it makes me so scared if these people get in office, and Donald J. Trump is the only one at this point who is fighting for what America truly stands for. That's how I feel about it."

Two miles down now. The sky was lightening. Other people were coming out. Bikers. Runners. Walkers. "Good morning," Michael called to them as they passed by.

"Are you a veteran?" one of them called back.

Maybe it was the wheelchair. Maybe it was the haircut.

"No, I'm an idiot," Michael said, not bothering to explain about the tree or any of it. He laughed his big, charming laugh, and the other person laughed, too, and then he was rolling on and serious again.

"I think Donald Trump is an American, freedom-loving man. I think that his family feels the same exact way. I think Donald Trump speaks his mind. Whenever he is hit, he hits back. You won't like everything that he says, but I haven't seen anything the man has said that was wrong. Everything that's come out of his mouth has been right . . ."

AS ENDLESS AS his thanks for Trump could be, his thanks for Ann were of an entirely different type. Trump may have been the one politician who spoke to him, but

Ann was the person who had salvaged him in that hospital bed, and of whom he had texted to Brent one day in early 2018 to say that she had been diagnosed with breast cancer. "She received the call yesterday," he had written. "We are at the cancer clinic now getting her first MRI so we will know exactly what we will be fighting."

She had gotten through it, but not easily. The surgeries were bad enough, but every difficulty was multiplied by the realities of a house with a C7 quad. For instance, Michael wasn't able to help her stand up, so she began sleeping in a recliner in the living room. They rearranged the kitchen so he could reach things. They figured out bathing. For four weeks, she wasn't supposed to raise her arms, so she bought an extra-large comb for Michael to help with her hair. There were a thousand things like that. The neighbors brought food, and she was grateful, but mostly she was frightened of dying, and she hurt.

And now she was back pretty much to how things had been beforehand, her fears fading, back to work, back to trying to get on the highway at five forty-five, before traffic got bad, and back to walking Scout around Pleasantville, where someone had posted on the listserv:

"I've noticed a few cars going past my house pretty fast, my estimate is between 30–40 mph."

". . . a white Subaru," someone else replied, mentioning one car in particular, "often at evening/early morning hours where it is harder to see both people and animals."

And isn't that the way it goes, Ann thought as she got into her white Subaru. One day you're getting food from your neighbors, and another day you're getting dimed out for trying to get to work on time and then home to your C7 husband.

She drove at 20 mph. She stopped at every stop sign. She was on her way to see her father who lived forty-five minutes away and seemed to be fading fast. One day, when she and Laura had been talking, Laura had asked her how she managed to take care of Michael, her parents, and all the sick people she nursed. "How do you do it?" she had asked. "You just keep doing it," Ann had answered, and now she was back to doing it, a sure sign she had recovered.

Her route took her around Atlanta rather than through it, and she was glad for that. Ten days before, there had been yet another police shooting of a black man. It had happened toward midnight at a Wendy's fast food restaurant just south of downtown in an area called Peoplestown. A twenty-seven-year-old man named Ray-shard Brooks had fallen asleep in his car in the drive-thru lane, and when the police tried to wake him, he was confused about where he was and appeared to be drunk.

"Okay. How much have you had to drink tonight?" one of the officers asked him.

"Not much," he'd answered.

"Not much? How much is not much?"

"About a drink," Brooks said.

"I'd just like to do some field sobriety tests," another officer said to Brooks a few minutes later. "Watch me while I demonstrate, okay? Keep your hands by your side. You're going to take a series of nine heel-to-toe steps counting them out loud. One, two, three. I took three steps. You're going all the way to nine . . ."

A few minutes later, Brooks took a breathalyzer.

"All right. Just take a deep breath in, put your mouth over the mouthpiece, blow as hard as you can until I tell you to stop," the officer told him. "Blow, blow, blow, blow, blow, blow, blow, blow, blow, blow . . ."

And a few minutes after that came an outcome far different from a DUI case in another part of Georgia, when an officer had said to Jesse Briggs, "All right, turn around for me, please," and Jesse had complied.

"All right. I think you've had too much to drink to be driving. Put your hands behind your back for me," one of the officers said to Brooks. "Put your hands behind your back. Hey, hey! Stop fighting. Stop fighting. Stop fighting. Stop fighting. You're going to get tased. You're going to get tased!"

"Stop, Mr. Rolfe," Brooks said to one of the officers. "Stop."

"Stop! You're going to get tased!"

"Mr. Rolfe."

"Hey! Hands off the fucking Taser!"

"Stop! Stop!"

"Hands off the Taser! Stop fighting! He got my fucking Taser."

It was all on audio and video—the fight, the three of them falling to the ground, an officer trying to tase Brooks, Brooks grabbing the Taser and firing one of its two charges at the officer, Brooks punching the other officer in the face and running, Brooks getting tased by that officer, Brooks turning and firing the Taser's remaining charge, the officer aiming his gun and firing three rapid shots, Brooks falling, Brooks dying.

Eighteen days before that, George Floyd had been killed in Minneapolis. Brooks's death wasn't that. It wasn't nine and a half minutes of a police officer kneeling on Floyd's neck and choking the life out of him while Floyd gasped "I can't breathe." But it was a dead man who a few minutes before had been an alive man saying "I just had a few drinks. That's it," and soon protesters were gathering, the Wendy's was on fire and burning to the ground, the Atlanta police chief was resigning, the medical examiner was calling Brooks's death a homicide, and the police officer who had fired his gun was being charged with felony murder.

After the George Floyd killing, downtown Atlanta had erupted. Windows had been smashed, stores looted, fires set, a state of emergency declared, the National Guard mobilized. That civil unrest, coupled now with the protests after Brooks's death, meant a city that to Ann was feeling increasingly tense. It wasn't only the city she could feel getting to her, though, it was all of it: COVID-19, her cancer, her dying parents, a feeling that social collapse was getting ever closer to Pleasantville itself. Was she the suburban woman whose fears Trump had been accused of stoking? Maybe so because every day she could feel her fears increasing.

Two-thirds of the way to her father's now, and she was passing a nursing care facility on her left that because of COVID was on lockdown. Nine residents had died so far and more were sick, and somewhere among them was her mother, whom she hadn't been able to see except through the window to her room. All of the windows had signs with room numbers on them now, so visitors making their way across the lawn and through the flowerbeds would know which window to stand at while they waved.

It was a helpful thing the home had done, but Ann wanted her mother out of there as soon as possible. Her dementia was causing balance issues, and Ann could see in video calls that her arms and hands were bruised from falls. Her mouth was bruised, too, from where she said someone had thrown a nurse-call button at her. Worse, the facility had a policy against the use of chair restraints, and the other day workers had found the poor woman pitched forward from her chair, leaning against a wall. No one had been able to tell Ann precisely what had happened, but it seemed her mother had been reaching to pick up something, maybe a cookie wrapper on the floor, and once again had lost her balance. She tipped forward, but instead of falling to the floor, she had been saved by the wall, against which she remained frozen until she was discovered. How long had she been there? No one could even guess.

"Hi, Mom," Ann said, calling her, and the voice on the other end of the line was so faint, Ann could barely hear her. "I know . . . I know . . . We're taking you home . . . It'll take some time . . ."

A few minutes later, she pulled in to the driveway of the house where her father now lived with Ann's son and his family. Her mother would be moving in too, as soon as her son could get the house ready. Of course she wished her mother and father could live with her and Michael, but that wasn't the way life worked.

How did it work? She was still figuring it out, but her

son's example was one possibility. For most of his life, he had been a mess: drugs, arrests, AWOL from the Army, homeless. He had been such a source of heartbreak, and yet here he was, drug-free at last, happy at last, ripping out carpets that would be like quicksand to someone in a wheelchair and putting in smooth floors. She couldn't have been prouder of the man he had become. So that was one way a life could work out, and another was Ann's own example: from the high hopes she had as a child, to failed marriages, to another relationship in which hot coffee had been thrown on her and one of her eyes had been blackened, to somehow the loveliness of Pleasant-ville with a man she considered the nicest man she had ever met. Until it happened, she'd never seen it coming, and now that it had she wanted to protect it from anyone trying to take it from her. She didn't want it to end.

"Hi, Dad," she said now, in the house, and when he didn't answer right away, she waited patiently until he did. He had dementia as well. A year ago, he had still been working. Now he was having dreams that were causing him to jump out of bed swinging at whatever he had been seeing.

"It's okay, Dad. You take your time," Ann said as he tried to explain his most recent dream to her.

"My dreams are—" he said, and then paused, lost. He sighed.

"Violent?" Ann asked.

"No."

"Bad?"

"No. Not violent," he said.

"That's good," she said.

"Last night I had a dream I can't understand."

"Were you in a fight?"

He didn't answer.

"Did you fall out of bed?"

He didn't say anything for five seconds, ten seconds, fifteen seconds, and then just said, "It's difficult."

"But you did good with that conversation," Ann said.

They were in the car now, headed to a doctor's appointment. Ann's phone rang, and the voice on the other end seemed to be coming from somewhere far away and underwater.

"Mom?" Ann said.

Exhales. Gasps, maybe. Something about a knee.

"Does it hurt?"

"Yes."

"Which knee? Left or right?"

Silence.

"Mom? Mom?"

"Yes?"

"Left knee or right knee?"

"Yes."

The line went dead. Her father started laughing.

"Can you imagine us together?" he said, suddenly lucid. "She can't think, and I can't speak."

They rode in silence, and then Ann mentioned a rally Trump had held two nights before.

"Dad, did you watch?"

"Part of it," he said.

"Did you get bored with it?"

"Yes," he said, and she confessed that she had, too, especially when Trump had gone on and on about why he had walked so carefully down a ramp after giving the commencement speech at West Point.

"I'm wearing leather-bottom shoes which is good if you're walking on flat surfaces. It's not good for ramps," he'd said.

"This was a steel ramp. It had no handrail, it was like an ice-skating rink . . ."

"I just saluted almost 600 times. I just made a big speech. I sat for other speeches. I'm being baked. I'm being baked like a cake . . ."

She never made it through the rest of Trump's speech, not the part where the crowd had chanted "Four more years! Four more years! Four more years! Four more years!" or, for that matter, any of the news coverage suggesting that the way he had shuffled down the ramp, and the way he'd had trouble taking a sip of water, needing both hands to steady the glass, might be indicative of health problems. Like Michael, she didn't pay attention to anything the mainstream media reported, only to AM talk radio, certain podcasts, and Fox News. And like Michael, she didn't need to watch a speech to know that she had grown to like Trump even more than she had loathed Hillary, or, now, Joe Biden, who a few weeks before had wrapped up the Democratic nomination.

There was nothing wrong with Donald Trump, not to her. He was a fighter, and she liked fighters. He was a man of his word, and after so many years in the company of men who lied to her, she liked men of their word. "I, Donald John Trump, do solemnly swear that I will faithfully execute the office of President of the United States and will, to the best of my ability, preserve, protect, and defend the Constitution of the United States so help me God," he had promised when he was inaugurated on January 20, 2017, and she wanted him to say those same words on January 20, 2021.

She wanted a president who would preserve, protect, and defend her Pleasantville life.

Now she told her father that Michael was sure Trump would win. "Hands down," she said.

Five seconds. Ten seconds.

"I am very nervous," she said.

"YEAH, TRUMP'S GOING TO WIN. I feel very confident," Michael was saying on another day, another roll.

He mentioned two polls he had seen—not one, which might be dismissible, but *two*—saying that 63 percent of Americans thought Joe Biden had dementia.

"I don't think people will vote for someone with dementia," he said, and then went on to describe what would happen if Biden did win:

"Biden is a hollow man. A Trojan horse."

"Soon after he gets in office, Biden will stand up and say, 'I cannot serve,' and his wife Jill will say, 'He cannot do this.'"

"Nancy Pelosi will take over. And Kamala Harris. AOC. Omar."

"You're going to have civil unrest. Gun buybacks, door to door. That's where the shooting starts. The stock market will plummet and 401(k)s will go down fifty percent. Taxes will go up astronomically. BLM and Antifa—they are going to have won."

"Biden's not going to be running the country. It's the radicals."

He kept going. The Green New Deal. A loss of U.S. manufacturing jobs. Windmills. Solar power. The end of coal. "Your electric bill would skyrocket. They want to eliminate cars. They want to make every car electric."

And one more: the loss of Christian values.

"Trump's the only one out there trying to protect American values," he said.

Before Trump, he wouldn't have been so certain in his opinions. He was reliably conservative—or, as he'd said one day, imagining Brent's politics, "the way I used to be"—but that changed in 2012, when President Obama announced a program that would keep some eight hundred thousand U.S.-born children of illegal immigrants from being deported. "Now let's be clear—this is not amnesty. This is not immunity. This is not a path to citizenship," Obama had said, and at first Michael thought of it as nothing other than an act of humanity. Over time, though, that shifted. It *was* amnesty, he realized, it *was* immunity, and it *was* a path to citizenship, and the point of it was to add all of those people to America's voting rolls, people who would vote for liberals and Democrats and bring about the end of conservatism. It wasn't humane at all. It was underhanded and nefarious, there was no other way to see it, and ever since then he looked at politicians differently, as devils and liars, all except for Trump.

More U.S. manufacturing, he said now of what would happen as a result of Trump's reelection. 401(k)s will grow. The First and Second Amendments will be protected. BLM, Antifa, the KKK, skinheads, and other extremist groups pushing for racial and ideological supremacy will be deemed terrorist organizations and their leaders will be rounded up and jailed.

"I feel very strongly. I love the United States. There are people now with radical ideas trying to change the country into something we are not, and it sickens me and disgusts me. It terrifies me," he said.

"All the fears I learned as a young man to watch out for are coming to fruition now."

It was a good workout this morning. Cool at the start and warm by the end, and if quadriplegia didn't come with the side effect of not being able to sweat, surely Michael would be sweating. He felt energized as he got in the van.

Before the pandemic, which he called "the plandemic," because he knew as surely as he knew anything that it was one more thing Democrats were hyping for political advantage, he might have run some errands. Maybe to Bass Pro Shops to see if any ammo had come in. So many people were stockpiling it now, afraid the government would be taking their guns and ammo away, the shelves were just about bare. Or maybe to Walmart, despite the sign on the door saying face coverings were mandatory. "Yeah, yeah, I'll subjugate for you," Michael had said the last time he was there, putting on a mask. "Do not ever think my kind nature is a weakness, because it isn't."

Instead, he headed home. Everything—everything—felt so fraught to him now because of the Democrats. "I don't think you know how big this world is," his father had said to him once. It was a mysterious sentence at the

time, but no longer. Lately, after seeing people at Trump
rallies holding QAnon signs, he'd been reading a little
about claims that the country, even the world, was under
the control of elitist, Satan-worshipping pedophiles. He
had little interest in QAnon and thought most of what its
believers were saying was nutty, like the wholesale kid-
napping of children and rituals involving the drinking of
their blood. But a few things gave him pause. He had no
doubt that pedophilia existed in Hollywood and that Sa-
tanists existed within the Democratic party. He also had
no doubt a deep state existed that was intent on over-
throwing Trump.

And there, in a nutshell, was his problem with Democrats. Because of the way they lied, who knew what was
true anymore in the big world his father had warned him
about? Really. Who knew?

"Come on, Scout," he said, home now, unstrapping
the bungee cord around his leg, opening the door, lowering the ramp.

The neighborhood was quiet. His street was quiet too,
including the house next door. Other than to wave, he
hadn't communicated with Brent since the day they'd
had that conversation, leaving both to wonder on their
own if anything they'd said had made an impression. Inside the house was the quietest place of all. Ann was away
for the day with her father. But she must have sensed he
was missing her, because here she was calling.

"Hi, baby," he said.

He listened as she told him about something she had
heard, that a famous singer had been tweeting insults

about Melania Trump, mocking her accent and calling her an illegal alien.

"That bitch," he said of the singer.

He kept listening.

"Yeah," he said, agreeing with her. "She does need to be stoned to death."

There just was no end to his love for Ann, and hers for him. One thing he loved was the fire in her that had gotten her through cancer and given them more time together, and one thing she loved was his courteousness, which caused him sometimes to apologize for using a cuss word, as he did now after hanging up and was back to thinking about Joe Biden.

"That mindless fucker—sorry—ain't going to win nothing," he said.

CHAPTER 8

"IT WAS LIKE the whole world was on fire," Brent's mother would sometimes tell Brent about 1968, the year he was born. There'd been the assassinations of Martin Luther King, Jr., and Robert F. Kennedy, Jr. There'd been race riots in a hundred cities across America, violence against antiwar protesters at the Democratic National Convention, Black Power protests at the Olympics, the invasion of Czechoslovakia by the Soviet Union, the Tet Offensive in Vietnam, and the deaths that year in Vietnam of seventeen thousand American troops—nearly fifty a day—the deadliest year of that war.

And yet the country had survived. That was her point, and now, five decades after such a year, Brent wanted to take faith in what she was saying, because America in 2020 felt to him like it might be heading toward something as bad as 1968, or worse.

If things felt fraught to Michael, to Brent, who was

now five months into being a civilian, they were feeling venomous.

"What a cesspool," he said one day of what he was seeing on his Twitter feed, which he was looking at constantly, even though it riled him up.

The attacks. The viciousness, and the megaphone aspect of it, too, not only from the extreme right but also from the extreme left, which he detested just as much. Tweets that were retweeted, and liked, and disliked, and argued about, and eventually reduced to arguments of: Fuck you. No, fuck *you.* "Everything is outrageous," Brent said of Twitter. "Well, no. *Not* everything is outrageous." But his feed made it seem so, insisting that he care about what happened in some grocery store express-checkout line, as if what seemed like a minor confrontation was of worldly significance. In a better world, he would have no interest in that whatsoever. He would know it was being blown out of proportion. And he *did* know that, but he also found himself caring, taking sides, having an opinion, becoming exasperated.

In Jerusalem, he had downloaded a meditation app at one point, hoping it would calm whatever was going on inside him. *Focus on your breathing,* it said, so he focused on his breathing. *Focus on the tip of your nose,* it said, so he focused on the tip of his nose. But then he would hear a bus go by and would think of the bus, and then he would think of the sound the tires made on the street and wonder if it was raining, and then the session would end and he would be back on Twitter reading something about Tucker Carlson and thinking, "Go fuck yourself."

The angry man—that was who he could feel himself becoming on many days, and then came night when the thing saying "Go fuck yourself" was his dream speaking to him.

Here, this night, for no discernable reason, it came again. He had gone to sleep early, after saying goodnight to Laura, Meredith, and Emily, who was home for the weekend, and all of a sudden he was awake and screaming.

"Did Emily hear?" he asked Laura the next day.

"Probably," Laura said. "She was awake. That's why she doesn't have friends sleep over."

"That's bullshit," Brent said.

"Brent, it's okay. It's okay," Laura said.

He tried to figure out what had triggered it. He used to think it was all tied to stress, as simple as that, but he'd had the dream after stress-free days, too. So it had to be something more specific. Was it because this day happened to be the anniversary of the second death in Iraq, the death that had made them all realize the first death wasn't a fluke, that there were going to be more?

There was a time when Brent knew every detail of every one of the deaths, but it had been thirteen years. The war that had first caused the dream was getting farther and farther away, and yet even as it receded, the dream persisted, immune to any attempt at rational explanation. Some days he barely thought of the war and had the dream, and then there were days he didn't have the dream and could have, like a day when he stumbled upon a photograph of a soldier who had taken his place one time in a convoy and ended up in the midst of explosion after explosion. Here was that soldier now, staring into a camera, not only sadder-looking than Brent had remembered him but also accompanied by a service dog, suggesting some lasting mental wounds. The guilt of that possibility tore Brent up. And yet that night, even after studying the photo, he didn't have the dream, so he doubted that the anniversary of a soldier's death, no matter what space it occupied in his subconscious, had caused this one.

Whatever the trigger, its effects were the same as always on Brent: the blackness, the mocking laughter, the feeling of being pulled in, the waking up terrified. Sometimes he would be able to get back to sleep. Sometimes he went downstairs. Sometimes he reached for his phone. Sometimes he looked at Twitter.

Here was an interesting one.

"Knowledge is power," it read. "It is important to know the history, but not to condemn for it."

It was about the county where he lived, and it was trending.

THE TWEET HAD TO DO WITH a protest that was going to take place later that day. It was going to be a Black Lives Matter protest in front of the county courthouse, part of a day of protests and marches taking place across the U.S. to honor the memory of George Floyd.

But it also was about progress and lack of progress in the county since 1987, when its black population was still zero, and on a cold day in mid-January, a busload of fifty people, some white, most black, had traveled north from

Atlanta for what had been intended as an interracial "Walk for Brotherhood."

It didn't last long. News accounts from that day said the marchers had made it about a third of the way along their planned two-and-a-half-mile route from the outskirts of town to the courthouse when a crowd of white people began chanting, "Go home, n——s," and attacked them with bottles, rocks, and fistfuls of mud. "I have never seen such hatred. There were youngsters ten and twelve years old screaming their lungs out, 'Kill the n——s,'" one of the organizers said afterward, stunned, while one of the haters said, "We sent a message today. We white people won and the n——s are on the run."

That wasn't the end, though, because a week later came a second attempt, and this time, because of national news coverage of the first march, a crowd estimated to be as large as twenty thousand people showed up. Led by Coretta Scott King, the widow of Martin Luther King, Jr., Andrew Young, the mayor of Atlanta, and other civil rights luminaries, they marched in a line more than a mile long.

Once again, white supremacists showed up, too, perhaps a thousand who again threw bottles and rocks, waved Confederate flags, and screamed racial obscenities. "We've got the best county up here; we've got the best lake," one of them said to a reporter, referring to nearby Lake Lanier, which the reporter pointed out was named after the Confederate soldier turned poet Sidney Lanier. "We'd like to keep it clear of black trash."

"Kill 'em all. Let God sort them out," one of their signs read, but this time a force of two thousand three hundred police officers and National Guard troops kept the two sides mostly apart, and the marchers made it all the way to the courthouse square.

Was that day in 1987 the day that the county began changing? People say it was, although thirty-three years later, it remained far from a settled place, as the tweets stacked up in Brent's feed about this day's Black Lives Matter protest were making clear. "I have no respect for blacks anymore because one thing is black lives don't matter" one of them read. And an email Brent was forwarded, with the subject line "Be aware!," warned, "The word is that the KKK will [be] at this gathering in full force."

The protest began in early afternoon of June 6, 2020, and a wide area of soft green grass in front of the county courthouse was soon filled with a thousand people. In some ways, it was 1987 all over again, but there were differences, too. In 1987, a police helicopter flew overhead; this day it was a drone. In 1987, a dominant chant was "N——s go home"; now, because of George Floyd and all of the other deaths of black men and women in police confrontations, it was "Prosecute police. Prosecute police." The courthouse was new, too; the old one, across the street, was now an annex and the office for the sheriff's department. A lot of deputies were patrolling the edges of the crowd, and some stood in front of the annex, listening to one of the protest speakers say, "Turn my mic up. I don't think they can hear my voice across the street." Into a turned-up microphone, crying now, she told of moving to the county thirteen years before, aware of the history but hopeful that the history was nothing more than that. "But it didn't take long for that to dissipate," she said. Her husband, she said, despite being the most careful of drivers, had so far been pulled over by deputies nine times.

"Where are you going?" she said, reciting what the deputies would ask her husband.

"Do you live in this neighborhood?"

"Where are you coming from?"

"Is this your car?"

And that was one thing the same as 1987, the sounds of genuine hurt and anger.

"But I'm here to tell you, black lives matter," the next speaker said, and meanwhile, at the edge of the crowd, a young black man with a sign in one hand that said, "Fuck the police," was holding his phone in the other hand and shooting a video of a white sheriff's deputy who was trying to ignore being humiliated. "Look at that belly," the young man said laughing, focusing on the deputy's stomach, and he continued laughing and videoing until an older black woman said to him, "That's not how we do it."

More deputies came over.

"How are you today?" the woman said to every one of them, and then she and the young man disappeared into a crowd of more black people than had lived in the county for almost the entirety of the previous century.

The afternoon went on, and maybe it was the shifting light, but even though the KKK never showed up, things began to feel more on edge.

"It's the knuckleheads in the north part of the county," a deputy said of who he was concerned about. "They've been here a long time, and they may be thinking, 'This is *our* area.'"

Now, on the road running in front of the courthouse, a car glided by with its windows down, exposing in the backseat a grinning white man who stuck his left hand out the window and balled it into a fist, showing off his brass knuckles.

"You be safe," a protester yelled at him. "You be safe."

Now a young black girl with a bottle of water in her hand ran full speed toward a white man who happened to be one of the protesters, and he flinched, knowing she was about to throw it at him. But she just shook some water onto him to cool him off against the summer heat, and he smiled as she ran away.

Now everyone was asked to kneel in silence, and except for the buzzing of the drone, everything went momentarily quiet and still. A minute passed. Two minutes. Three. Four.

A car rolled past.

"Fuck you," the driver yelled. "Fuck you! Fuck you!"

Five minutes. Six. Seven. Eight. Now George Floyd was dead, and everyone rose to their feet.

"Thank you," the person at the microphone said.

BRENT, MEANWHILE, was out running errands that day, and when he walked into the house late in the afternoon, Laura and Emily were at the kitchen table, talking about an online test Laura had just taken at Emily's urging. It was called the Implicit Association Test, and it was supposed to reveal a person's hidden biases by measuring re-

sponse times to a series of pictures and words. The one
Laura had taken was about race, and it had shown flash-
ing images of black people and white people and words
such as "lovely," "nasty," "hatred," and "beautiful."

"What kind of test is that, though?" Brent asked.

"You should take it," Emily said.

"You should," Laura said.

"But let's say I have a slight preference for black people," Brent said. "Is that good? Is that weird?"

"You should take it," Laura said again. "I had a moderate preference."

"Toward whites?" Brent asked.

"I was surprised," Laura said.

"I mean I'm sure those things have some merit," Brent
said. "But—"

"I retook it and got no preference one way or the
other," Laura said.

"But you knew what you were doing that time," Emily
said.

"But it was in a different order," Laura said and then
asked if there were others they could take. "For Asians?
For Mexicans?"

"Mexicans?" Brent said.

"Hispanics," Laura said, correcting herself.

"Mexicans?" Brent said again.

"Hispanics," Laura said again. "Aren't they the largest minority in the U.S.? More than African Americans?"

"I don't think so," Brent said.

"Let's ask Alexa," Laura said.

They didn't ask Alexa, which kept a record of everything they did ask—what's the weather forecast, set a

timer for eight minutes, play some Judah & the Lion—
but a few nights later, they picked up the conversation
again. This time it began after Laura mentioned that
when she saw people, she didn't see skin color, just people, and Emily told her that wasn't a good thing to say.

"That's like saying 'I don't see color, I see everyone as
equal,'" Emily informed her. "But if you see everyone as
equal, you're not recognizing where the disparities are,
and where the differences are, and where there needs to
be room for growth. If you truly don't see color and think
that everyone is equal, then you don't see where the problems with everything are. You don't see where a black
person, from birth, is already way far behind—"

"So am I supposed to treat a black person that I meet
different than I treat a white person, or do I treat them
the same?" Laura asked.

"You treat them the same," Emily said. "Obviously.
And I'm not saying that *you* don't. That's not what I was
trying to get at. I was just saying that's not necessarily
the correct way to say that. That's what I was trying to
get at."

"But, again, when I said I don't see color, it's not that
I don't recognize it," Laura said.

"I know. I know," Emily said.

"That wasn't the intent," Laura said. "The point that
I was making was I'm not going to treat somebody of
color different than I'm going to treat somebody that's
white, or somebody that's brown or somebody that's Indian, that's not who I am."

"I know. And that's good," Emily said. "I'm just
pointing out that that is not the way to phrase it."

"Okay," Laura said. "I won't phrase it like that again."

"I don't know. All this microaggression stuff is hard to understand," Brent said.

"Yeah," Emily said. "The way I think about it is that I was in a class, and we had to read this article about white privilege. And I'm in a class of predominantly white females, and one of the microaggressions listed was that the lady who had written the article, who was a black woman, had been followed in a store. And the girls in my class are saying, 'Oh, I've been followed at the mall,' 'I've been followed around in a store,' 'I've been followed by a creepy man like leering at me in the store,' and not realizing—"

"Oh!" Laura yelled suddenly.

"What?" Brent said.

"Mittens!" Laura said, not to Brent but to the cat, which was going to the bathroom on her foot.

"Put her outside!" Brent said.

"Oh, Mittens," Laura said.

"Not realizing," Emily continued, "that what the lady in the article was talking about was being followed by the store employees who thought that she was going to steal something. So that's what I look at as a microaggression. It was a lot of white students and our African American teacher, and the white students are saying, 'Well, I've had the same experience.' But then our African American teacher could tell the story of when she went to the Cracker Barrel and got followed around and called the store employees out for being like, 'You're not following this white lady over here, you're not following that white guy over there,' and so it's like that."

"I understand. That makes sense," Brent said. "Where it gets dicey is like, Why do people follow you? What is it? Race? Or what? What do people see?"

"Well, I can tell you from having a friend who worked at a Victoria's Secret who told me that when a black person walked in the store they would come over the headset and specifically say, 'We have friends in the store,' that yes, it is about race, at least for that specific store."

And it went on from there, until at one point Brent decided to let Emily in on something that had been happening to him.

He had just learned of a petition to get the organization he worked for kicked out of the university where it was located. It was a petition branding the work as racist, and, by extension, Brent realized, him as a racist, too.

"I haven't told you, but two hundred faculty members at my university—" he began.

"Yeah, Mom showed me," Emily said.

"Yeah," Brent said, and here was another version of genuine hurt and anger.

WHEN HE FIRST heard of the petition, he was in the midst of writing something about George Floyd for the website of the organization that had hired him as its associate director, the Georgia International Law Enforcement Exchange, or GILEE. It was an organization that since 1992 had trained nearly two thousand U.S. police officers in community policing, primarily through an exchange program with Israeli police. For two weeks at a time, small groups of American police officers would travel around Israel and see how their counterparts used community policing and counterterrorism techniques to keep things under control, and, in return, Israeli police delegations would come to the U.S. for similar tours.

That association with Israel was the basis for the criticism of GILEE, which came primarily from organizations promoting Palestinian statehood and civil rights. To them, the lessons American police officers were learning in Israel, and bringing back to their American police departments, had to be lessons in how to restrict civil liberties and commit human rights violations, the kinds of lessons that might lead a police officer to blithely kneel on someone's neck until he was dead. The criticisms of GILEE never came with direct proof, only implications, but the petition was the first time Brent had experienced it, and it came just as he had written, "We join all who mourn for George Floyd and his family. His brutal killing at the hands of four Minneapolis police officers is an egregious example of the abuse of police power, reverberating worldwide."

He'd continued: "The abuse of power by law enforcement officers is unacceptable on all counts: morally, legally and professionally. It carries with it the loss of trust and is counterproductive to the ideals behind the provision of professional and ethical police service to the community . . ."

And then, suddenly, instead of writing, he was reading a letter that had been sent to the president of Georgia State University, where GILEE had its offices.

"We are writing this letter both as members of the Black community and as faculty members at Georgia

State University," it began, and then offered its own interpretation of GILEE.

"We live the experience of being Black in America, and in that regard submit this letter as an expression of solidarity with those who are using their bodies in visceral objection to the murders of Ahmaud Arbery, Breonna Taylor, George Floyd, and countless other victims of racial violence whose lives did not matter to some."

"There is a clear historical record of white supremacy that is an animating aspect of this nation and of the State of Georgia."

"Georgia State University sits in the heart of Atlanta, Georgia, America's citadel of civil rights."

"And though the city embraces the sobriquet 'The City Too Busy To Hate,' and its civic identity is inextricably intertwined with the life and legacy of its native son, Dr. Martin Luther King, Jr., it is no stranger to police violence resulting in the death of Black people."

"We are therefore alarmed by Georgia State University's police exchange program, which partners with international law enforcement agencies that restrict civil liberties, commit human rights violations, and/or promote bigotry, signaling an aggressive, militarized overpolicing of Black people and Black communities."

"The University must divest from this program immediately . . ."

And then came signatures, a lot of them. Brent looked at them, counted them and realized they amounted to ten percent of the entire faculty.

"If ten percent of our colleagues think we're doing something illegal, unethical, and immoral, that's disturbing," he said to his boss, Robbie Friedmann, during a phone call about the letter. It was Friedmann, a criminology professor, who'd started GILEE when Atlanta was about to host the 1996 summer Olympics. With clear memories in mind of the 1972 Olympics, when Palestinian militants kidnapped and killed eleven Israeli athletes, Friedmann, who'd been raised in Israel, got Israeli officials he knew to share with Atlanta officials some of the things they had learned over the years about preventing terrorism, and the program had grown from there.

By now, Friedmann was used to the attacks on GILEE that would come up from time to time because of its ongoing affiliation with Israel, and he tried to assure Brent that this one would blow over, just as the others had. For one thing, the president of the university, the person who'd received the letter, had just named GILEE the winner of its annual award for community service and social justice. For another, GILEE's website was loaded with testimonials, including one from Andrew Young, the former Atlanta mayor and civil rights luminary who said in his endorsement of GILEE, "We have a responsibility to develop a science of civility that allows us to live together as brothers and sisters lest we perish together as fools."

"I somehow hope this will end up well," Friedmann said. "How do I put this? I want to be soberly optimistic."

"Sounds good to me," Brent said, adding, "Better than drunkenly optimistic."

But when he hung up, he wasn't persuaded at all.

"I'm getting pissed," he said. "This is bullshit. It angers me."

What was that lesson about focusing on his breathing?

"I've never been accused of racism," he said. "And now two hundred people automatically think I'm a racist."

What was the lesson about focusing on the tip of his nose?

He kept hearing the words, *You're a racist*. "I get a little emotional because I can't say anything back," he said.

He decided to say something back.

He started writing again. This time it was a letter to the two hundred people.

"I know what you think. Now let me tell you something about me," was what he wanted to write, but instead he took a less combative tone. "My peers at the University didn't attempt to reach out to GILEE and didn't ask for conversation or discussion," he wrote, and then told them what they would have learned if they had.

"I think these signatories would be surprised to learn of the diversity of GILEE, which is one-third female and two-thirds foreign born," he said as a way to introduce them to the staff they hadn't taken the opportunity to meet: a Romanian-born man who'd been raised in Israel, a woman born in Belarus when it was still part of the USSR, and a man who'd spent twenty-eight years serving his country.

"I believe they would be surprised that I spent over three and a half years deployed away from my family training the Palestinian Authority Security Forces across the West Bank in the rule of law and human rights, and that I talk almost weekly with friends in Palestine and fondly remember my shared Iftar dinners," he wrote—and wondered how many of the two hundred had been to an Iftar dinner.

"I proudly display my awards from my Palestinian Authority colleagues in my home and office."

And how many of them had such an award?

"I bring this point forward because as a retired officer I would not join or participate in an organization that didn't fully respect rule of law and human rights," he continued, more and more fired up. "These concepts are ingrained in me, and the Army values I lived by, and continue to live by, do not allow me to participate in an organization that would in any way threaten our communities or discriminate against African Americans or anyone."

That's a pretty good letter, he thought when he had finished, except for two things.

First, how should he sign it? In the Army, everything was signed "Very respectfully" or V/R, but he wasn't feeling a whole lot of respect at the moment.

And second, should he send it?

He wasn't sure.

A FEW WEEKS LATER, there was another demonstration, this one in a park near downtown Atlanta.

"When I say 'fuck,' you say 'police'!" someone yelled into a bullhorn to a few dozen people who had gathered for the demonstration, and to anyone passing by, it might have seemed like another antipolice demonstration.

"Fuck!"

"Police!"

"Fuck!"

"Police!"

But now came a new chant.

"When I say 'abolish,' you say 'GILEE'!" the speaker yelled.

"Abolish!"

"GILEE!"

"Abolish!"

"GILEE!"

"Abolish!"

"GILEE!"

It was a beautiful late afternoon. People on bicycles, on scooters, on rollerblades rolled past, pausing to listen. More people showed up, including someone holding a sign that said GILEE IS A TERRORIST ORGANIZATION, and someone else who was surreptitiously taking a video.

"We want to educate about GILEE, and raise awareness, so we can shut it down," the woman with the bullhorn yelled.

"Shut it down!" people yelled back.

"GILEE is responsible for Israeli militarized police teaching and for training Atlanta police departments, as well as Ferguson, Minneapolis, and most major cities in America, how to kill black and brown bodies," she said. "This is not okay."

"Not okay!" a few people repeated.

Was she right? It didn't matter. As an adviser to Donald Trump had once declared, two days into his presidency and setting up all that was to come, alternative facts were facts, too, and to the people listening to the woman with the bullhorn, and now clapping, she was absolutely right, and they were ready to yell again when she prompted them with "Abolish!"

"GILEE!"

"Abolish!"

"GILEE!"

More applause as another speaker took the bullhorn.

"Dr. King said an injustice anywhere is a threat to justice everywhere," he said. "You cannot separate the injustices in America from the injustices in Palestine. It is the same evil wicked system of genocide and apartheid under white supremacy. The resistance in Gaza and the West Bank is very similar to that here in America. We have people of color living in these de facto colonies and being oppressed and exploited. Living under militarization whether it's the Israeli Army or the Atlanta police department. And this can be proven by the program of GILEE. So you take police from Atlanta and send them to Israel to train. Israel with its thousands if not millions of human rights violations. It's almost as if America said, 'Teach us how to kill these people of color faster. Teach us how to oppress black folks more than we already do . . .'"

More applause, more cheers, more chants.

"Black lives . . ."

"Matter!" the crowd yelled in response.

"Black lives . . ."

"Matter!" people yelled, and as the chants continued, two men in the crowd, both of whom were black, began arguing with each other.

"Viva, viva, Palestina," the woman yelled into the bullhorn.

"Viva, viva, Palestina," the crowd yelled back.

Now one of the men dropped a backpack he was carrying and moved closer to the other.

Now the other dropped his backpack and raised his fist.

Someone tried to get between them. "These are your people," he said to both of the men, reminding them of who they were, but it was too late.

One swung and hit the other in the face.

"Black man, back up!" the man who'd tried to intervene yelled. "Black man, back up," but both were swinging fists now.

"This is why white people—" the man yelled, but whatever else he was saying got lost in the chants.

"From the river to the sea, Palestina will be free . . ."

The man was imploring them. "Black people fighting black people over stupid shit."

"From the river to the sea, Palestina will be free," the crowd chanted, and at each pause came the thud of fists hitting skin.

"I'm yelling at you," the man yelled, trying to separate them. "I'm yelling at you."

More blows. Harder. Louder. The fight was turning brutal.

"Don't you get it?" the man yelled.

The two men were on the ground now. More swings. More thuds.

"Don't you get it? Don't you get it? Don't you get it?

You don't get it!" the man yelled, his chant mixing with the others.

He tried again to pull them apart, and now some other people helped, and at last the fight came to an end, the demonstration eventually fizzled out, and everyone left, including the person who'd taken the video, which soon made its way to GILEE, and to Brent, who watched it and decided not to send his letter.

Because, he said, what would be the point? Who was going to hear him?

EVERYTHING WAS FRAYING. That's what it felt like.

He watched a clip of a Trump rally in Wisconsin.

"We are going to win four more years," Trump said.

"Four more years! Four more years!" the crowd chanted.

"And then after that, we'll go for another four . . ." and as the crowd cheered, Brent thought: *Why are they cheering? Have these people read the Constitution? Ever?*

He watched clips of windows being smashed and fires being set in downtown Atlanta after another police shooting; of Black Lives Matter demonstrators surrounding some people eating outside a restaurant in Washington, D.C., and trying to intimidate them into raising their fists in solidarity; of protesters in Portland marching along a residential street at midnight and shouting, "Wake up, motherfucker, wake up! Wake up, motherfucker, wake up!"

He went with Laura to Costco, where a worker approached a woman with a dangling mask and told her that because of COVID, she needed to pull the mask up over her mouth and nose.

"I don't like your demeanor," the woman said.

"Sorry. It's just the policy," the worker said.

"Well, this is ridiculous!" the woman said, raising her voice. "How am I supposed to drink my water with a mask on?" She yanked up her mask, raised a bottle of water she was holding, poured it out over her mask and clothing, and yelled, "Is this what you want?"

"We cannot have four more years," Laura said on a day when Trump was sending out another barrage of tweets, forty-one in all.

. . . AMERICA FIRST! . . .

. . . SLOW JOE . . .

. . . MAKE AMERICA GREAT AGAIN! . . .

"I really want someone to tell him that for every all-caps tweet he sends out, he will lose a thousand heart-beats," Laura said.

It was nighttime now. It started to rain and Brent went out onto his front porch. All during his time in Iraq, he'd held on to a vision of what would be waiting for him after the war, and a porch was always part of the deal, along with his dog, a beer, and a rainstorm. Yes, it was sentimental, but to a man who had been scared some-times and often lonesome, it had seemed a version of life worth defending.

"You okay?" Laura had once asked him during the war, when he'd come home on leave. They were living in Kansas then, and Brent had awakened to the sound of explosions. Just thunder, he'd realized, so he'd gone out-side to see his first rainstorm in months. He'd watched the lightning flashes come closer. He'd felt the air turn damp. The rain, when it came down on the roof, and fell through the downspouts, and washed across his lawn, and flowed along his street, had felt cleansing, and he was hoping it would wash through him too.

"Yeah, just watching the storm," he'd said to Laura.

He'd also gone to a coffee shop when he was home, where one of the regulars clapped him on the back and motioned to one of the other regulars. "Come on over and meet Brent Cummings," he'd said. "He's just back from Iraq. He's a hero." Brent had winced at the word, but the idea of sitting in a coffee shop, reading the paper and talking about the world with a bunch of regulars who might disagree on some things but always agreed on how good the coffee was, appealed to him in its civility, and it became part of his vision of life after the war.

If only things had worked out that way. Instead, Laura's wish apparently wasn't coming true, because the latest tweet from the president of the United States said, "Don't buy GOODYEAR TIRES—They announced a BAN ON MAGA HATS. Get better tires for far less!"

Brent called an old college friend of his named Dan and asked if he had seen the tweet.

"What's the big deal?" Dan said. "So what?"

"The problem is you have the president of the United States injecting himself into private company business and affecting the stockholders' share value by tweeting about it," Brent said.

"We don't want to affect the rich white people!" Dan said.

"But it hurts the workers, and it hurts their pension plan, the blue-collar pension plan workers of Goodyear," Brent said.

"Look, I'm with you," Dan said. "I'm with you."

"So why would you vote for him?"

"Because I don't trust Biden," Dan said.

"But you trust Trump?" Brent said. "You've seen what Trump has done."

"Hang on. I'm getting a call," Dan said. "I'll call you back."

Dan hung up. Brent was pretty sure he wouldn't be calling back.

Breathe.

Tip of nose.

He called one of his old soldiers.

"Hey, man, how are you? It's Brent."

"Hey, sir," the soldier said.

"A little thunderstorm going on here," Brent said in case the soldier was hearing explosions.

It was a big thunderstorm, but Brent stayed on the porch anyway. The soldier wanted to know what life was like after the Army, and they talked about the meaning of what they had done, and the value of it. "And then boom," Brent said. "All that goes away. You know? 'What am I going to do today?' You know? So it's just a weird, a weird anxious feeling. Or at least it was for me." "Hey, sir. Thanks," the soldier said at the end of the conversation. "Be safe, man," Brent said, and ten minutes later, he was still on the porch listening to the rain. Here came a car, lighting up the road, turning in to the driveway next door,

Ann, home from another day of nursing the broken. The garage door opened. The garage door closed. Everything was dark again. More thunder. It was turning into one of those nights. He didn't want to go to sleep because he knew the dream would be waiting, and the reason it would be waiting was because he was thinking now about what all of them had been through, including the day he almost died under the fuel truck. The day he almost died when he was waiting for his laundry. The day he almost died in the mortar attack that blew out his window. The day he almost died in the rocket attack that decapitated a contractor. The day he almost died in another rocket attack, when the chaplain was in the midst of giving him a haircut. The day he almost died when a roadside bomb exploded just after his Humvee had passed where the bomb had been buried. The day he almost died, which had been every day. Fourteen months in Iraq and twenty-eight years in the Army, all in the name of defending democracy, and now he wasn't defending it, he was in it, just in time to feel it unravel.

ONE STRATEGY HE had learned was waking up early. If he could wake up before the dream began, he would be fine, a little tired but fine, which was why he didn't mind at all being in his truck now at four in the morning, headed with his dog Finn to a competition to see what kind of bird dog Finn was turning into.

For months, Brent had been training Finn, usually at Lake Lanier, the reservoir that in 1987 that white racist had said he wanted to keep "clear of black trash." Thirty-three years later, Brent would get to the lake by driving through a neighborhood where Trump signs had remained staked into front yards long after the 2016 election. It was a beautiful part of the lake, especially at daybreak, when Brent preferred to go. The air was still damp. The water was just beginning to light up. No one else was around. No phone, no Twitter, just Brent and Finn. "Finn. Dead bird," Brent would say and direct Finn into the lake and toward a shoreline a hundred yards away, where Brent had hidden a decoy at the base of a pine tree. "Good dog," he'd say when Finn returned it to him and dropped it at his feet, as if delivering a bird Brent had shot out of the sky. "Good boy," he'd say and send Finn back out again.

It had been Laura who had selected Finn from a litter of newborn puppies because Brent at that point had been in Jerusalem. There had been three puppies running around, and three sets of owners who had drawn straws to see who would get the first choice, and Laura had won. Why couldn't she have lost, she had thought, so she wouldn't have the pressure of choosing? Why couldn't Brent have been there to choose?

"How'd you end up picking him?" he'd asked when he called afterward, looking at a photograph she had sent.

"The other two were wrestling around," she'd told him. "I almost went for the one that was kind of mouthy, wanted to pick up a lot of things and carry them around. But this one came over to Meredith and I. He really came up to Meredith first thing—"

"He picked us," Brent had said.

"What?" Laura had said, not hearing.

"Good job," Brent had said. "He's a cutie."

Now, months later, Brent had transformed Finn into a formidable dog.

The competition was in Tennessee, and to get there Brent headed west for a while and then north through the part of Georgia where the Republican nominee for the U.S. Congress was the far-right conspiracy theorist Marjorie Taylor Greene. Somewhere out there among the churches and gun shops were the forty-three thousand eight hundred thirteen people who had voted for her in the primary, but it was too dark to see anything about them other than their lit-up billboards and gas stations, and by the time the sun was coming up, he was at the event in Tennessee, among several hundred people who were gathered in a field waiting for a judge to call out the words "Guns up!"

Someone blew a duck call, a dead mallard was flung into the air as if it were flying, a gun was fired as if it contained ammo rather than blanks, the mallard fell as if it had been hit, and a dog who had been watching all this and listening to it all raced to get it.

Next dog.

Next dog.

"You ready to work?" Brent asked Finn.

There were dogs everywhere, ready to spend the day retrieving ducks. There were pickup trucks everywhere, too, mostly Fords and Chevys, and chewing tobacco, and vapes, and beards on almost every man, and a woman with the weariest of eyes who sat in a chair with a cigarette dangling from the side of her mouth, focused on a sheet of paper covered in dog names that she was marking up as if she was at a horse track. It would be easy enough to assume things about every one of these people, but just as Brent didn't want people assuming things about him, he wasn't going to do that to them. No one was talking about politics anyway, just dogs, and everyone seemed happy to be where they were and doing what they were doing, even the bird boys, which was the term for the boys and girls who when signaled to do so would heave a dead mallard into a field of dew and ticks.

Brent waited patiently, Finn at his side whimpering a little. "Shhh. Shhh," Brent said to him. Good dogs didn't whimper, and Brent knew Finn was a good dog. What he wanted was for everyone to know that. He wanted Finn to do so well that when he took off running toward a dead duck, people would stop talking and watch in amazement.

For now, though, they were talking and talking. "Hey, what's that story Jerry Clower used to tell about a big old bull?" one of them said and then proceeded to tell the story like Jerry Clower himself used to tell it at the Grand Ole Opry: "There are three bulls, an old one, a regular one, and a young one, and they're standing around, overlooking a field full of cows, when they overhear the farmer tell one of the cowhands to get the trailer ready to pick up a new bull. The old bull snorts and says, 'I'm telling you what, there are fifty cows here that are mine and if that new bull thinks he's getting any of my cows, he's got another think coming.' The second bull says, 'There ain't but thirty cows here that are mine but that new bull ain't getting any of my cows.' The young bull says, 'There ain't but ten cows here that even know me, but I sure ain't letting that new bull have any of 'em.' A few hours later a tractor trailer arrives and the trailer doors open and the gate lowers and out comes what has to be the biggest, meanest, orneriest-looking Brahman bull they've ever seen. Great big hump on his back, huge horns, froth dripping from his jowls as he stamps and paws at the ground. The old bull says, 'You know, I've been thinking, it's mighty selfish of me to keep all them cows for myself, I might just part with a few to be neighborly.' The second bull says, 'You know, I'm thinking the same thing, no need for me to keep all thirty of them cows to myself.' The young bull lets out a huge snort and starts stamping and pawing at the ground, raising a huge ruckus. The old bull says, 'Woo boy, what's the matter with you? Don't you know that new bull will kill you?' The young bull says, 'I'm just making sure that he knows that I'm a *bull* . . .' "

Even the woman smoking the cigarette laughed.

"That's a good one," someone said, and Brent was reminded of how nice people could be, especially if he didn't think about them in political terms.

Finn's turn.

No one stopped talking—the story now was about a grandchild who got bacterial meningitis; the possibility of an amputation; a coma for five days; no amputation; completely healthy; a miracle; thanks be to God and Jesus Christ—but they did watch.

"Nice job," one of them said to Brent.

"Thank you," he said.

Finn was panting.

"Good boy," Brent said to him and listened in as the

talk moved on to the next dog in line to go, whose name
was Liberty.

"Because she was born on the Fourth of July," said the
cigarette woman.

"That's a good name," Brent said.

"Liberty," the woman said. "A lot of people don't
know what that means anymore."

"Especially the younger ones," said a man who hadn't
been one of the younger ones in many, many years. "When
you got three uncles shot up in World War Two, you
know."

*Or when you almost die while waiting for your laun-
dry,* Brent didn't say, not out loud.

"Good job," was what he did say, about Liberty, who
hadn't done as well as Finn. He could be nice, too.

Hours later, back in his truck, back to thinking again
about politics as he passed through the part of Georgia
that according to every prediction would soon belong to
Marjorie Taylor Greene in a landslide, he was on the
phone with his friend Dan.

"If President Trump called you up and asked you out
to dinner, would you go?"

"Would I go?" Dan said. "Hell yeah."

"I don't know if I would go or not," Brent said. "It'd
be hard."

"Well, of course it would be hard," Dan said, who
knew by now, over and over, what Brent thought of
Trump. "Because you'd *want* to—"

"I'd want to," Brent agreed. "But you've heard what I
said. I think he's—"

"Yeah," Dan interrupted. "Blah blah blah blah blah."

"—not following the oath of the Constitution," Brent continued.

"How is he not following the Constitution?" Dan asked.

"Well, you know, support and defend the Constitution of the United States against all enemies foreign and domestic and to bear true faith and allegiance to the same," Brent said. "I think—"

"Yeah?"

"—he has lied."

"Oh God. Blah blah blah, blah blah blah."

"I mean you asked me," Brent said. "I'm telling you. You know morality-wise, he's having an illicit relationship while his wife is pregnant with his last child, and then he might have used campaign funds to help pay it off. Which is being investigated. So that's morality. Ethically, he asked a foreign nation to—"

"Blah blah blah blah," Dan said. "Please. Stop."

"What?"

"Just *stop*."

That was in August.

In September, with the election two months away now, Brent told Laura he had a feeling something bad was going to happen. "I think between now and November, there's a chance for significant violence," he said. He didn't know what or where, but he did have an idea of who: "the Tim McVeigh folks." The reference was to a soldier who had been at Fort Riley just before Brent had gotten there for the first time early in his career, in the same unit he would join, in the same company even, who after leaving the Army one day loaded a rented truck with explosives, parked it outside of a federal office in Oklahoma City, and detonated it, killing one hundred sixty-eight people, nineteen of them children. McVeigh was eventually executed for what he had done, and it was his successors Brent worried about now, the 2020 versions of an enraged, grievance-filled, white supremacist and domestic terrorist. He and Laura had been talking lately about getting an AR-15, which was so close to the M4 Brent had used in Iraq that he could take it apart and put it back together in the dark. Maybe this was the time to finally get one, he said, and in that moment the idea of bedside wasp spray seemed almost quaint.

October now, and he was on the phone again with Dan.

"People are already voting down there?" Dan asked.

"Yeah, yeah, we've been voting since Monday. We've had record-breaking numbers," Brent said. "It's mostly being led by Democrats, it seems, but we'll see. But people have been standing as long as eight hours in line to vote."

"Really?" Dan said.

"Yeah, they're getting it done."

"Well that's interesting because all those people are closet Trump supporters," Dan said.

"They might be," Brent said. "There's a lot of Trump signs down here."

"It'll be very interesting," Dan said.

"It will be. It will be. We will see what happens," Brent said.

"Do you think Biden will concede defeat?" Dan said.

"Yeah, I think if he gets beat, he would. I think he's actually on the record as saying so. Unlike his opponent," Brent said. "Which is kind of interesting."

"Who would have thought?" Dan said. "You know, we saw him when we grew up, he was on those talk shows with David Letterman or whatever. Who thought he was going to somehow become president?"

"Exactly," Brent said. "That's a problem."

"I agree," Dan said. "I mean it's like Bizarro World."

"Yeah," Brent said.

CHAPTER 9

ON THE FIRST DAY of early voting, the line outside the county elections office was so long that a volunteer poll worker decided a joke would be just the thing to make the wait feel shorter. "Are you in the mood for a little humor?" he asked, and before anyone could answer, he was telling a story about Billy Graham flying home from preaching, being picked up by a limo service, asking if he could drive because he'd never driven a limo, and getting pulled over for speeding by a trooper who saw him, got flustered, and called his supervisor. "'I need to know what to do because I've stopped a very important person.' 'Is it the president?' 'No.' 'Is it a celebrity?' 'No.' 'Well, who is it?' 'Well, it must be Jesus Christ because Billy Graham is the chauffeur.'"

Big, big laughs. There wasn't much doubt about how the vote was going to go in a place where a car now pulling in to the parking lot had a bumper sticker that read HILLARY FOR PRISON 2016.

"It's changing—but it's not changed," another poll worker said about the county, and as lines of voters continued to grow at every polling place, one of the people waiting in line was Laura.

She was by herself and hoping the line would move quickly because of something her mother had said the day before. "I'm tired," she had said. "I'm just tired. There's nothing more I can do in my life." She was too exhausted to get out of bed, down to a few bites of mashed potatoes a day.

So she was dying, at long last. It probably wouldn't be today, but Laura needed to get back to her. "Are you leaving?" her mother had asked at the end of the previous day's visit, when Laura had gotten up to go, and she was hearing those words, the need in them, as she inched her way forward. It took an hour, but at last she was inside, voting for, as she described it, "democracy, the rule of law, decency," and then she was hightailing it to her mother, to Meredith, and back to her mother again.

Two days later, Meredith turned eighteen, and when Laura got her mother on the phone to say happy birthday, her mother said, "Happy birthday, Emily," and then asked Laura if she could bring her some oranges. "Mandarin oranges," she said.

Laura started looking around the cabinets. Somewhere, in one of them, was one of those plastic cups of mandarin oranges, the kind packed in light syrup that when she was growing up had seemed so exotic to her. Where was it?

Here came Brent, in with the dinner Meredith had asked for, a hamburger, no bun because of gluten, extra pickles because she liked pickles. "I asked for extra pick-les, and you got 'em!" Brent said, unwrapping it for her. "Yay!"

Meredith smiled at him.

"Mer," Laura said a few minutes later, "are you going to want a cupcake tonight, or is your tummy full?"

Meredith looked up from her plate.

"Is your tummy full?"

Another birthday, another year of a life lived mostly in silence.

"You want a cupcake tonight or tomorrow?"

"Tonight," Meredith said.

"Tonight? All right. Let me set things up," Laura said.

She set things up. Everyone sang. Meredith blew out the candle. There was her smile again. Everyone clapped. Laura found the mandarin oranges, and then she was off to see her mother, to help her eat the oranges.

Two days after that, her mother spoke for the last time, when Laura brought Meredith to say goodbye.

"I love you," said the girl who didn't talk to anyone to a woman who for a day now had been saying only the word "water."

"I love you, Meredith," her grandmother said, clear as a bell, and then said nothing more after that.

Laura took Meredith home and hurried back. One of her sisters was there, too, and they took turns soaking a sponge in water and running it across their mother's lips. Laura looked at how dry they were becoming. She looked at her mother's arms, at how they were stiffening against her body, and at her hands and fingers, which were begin-ning to lose color and curl.

Four years before, when Laura had been with her father as he died, she had played music for him. He had
loved opera, but he hadn't raised Laura to like it, so she
went with church hymns, which he had also liked, until it
was clear he just wanted quiet. That quiet then was this
quiet now, and as it stretched on, Laura kept looking at
her mother and considering what a life added up to. How
many books had her mother read? How many places had
she traveled, as far away as Nepal? There was the work
she had done with the League of Women Voters, trying
to get the Equal Rights Amendment passed, and the years
she had volunteered as a poll worker in elections. And
there was the house she had never wanted to leave, where
she had raised four daughters and which for some reason
had come with a bomb shelter. The surprises of a life. All
that had happened. And then came the rest of what a life
turns out to be. Eventually you leave the house you never
wanted to leave. Eventually you become a ninety-year-old
in a single bed, eyes closed and out of words and listening
to the sounds of your daughter as she gets up from the
sofa and starts sorting through all of the things you're
about to leave behind.

Here, buried in a drawer, Laura found the wallet her
mother kept saying was lost.

Here, in the refrigerator, was a cupcake from her
birthday a month before and a container of curdled milk.

Here, for some reason, was a church bulletin from a
church in Topeka. Here were some menus. Mail. Magazines. There was so much stuff. Laura kept digging.

Here was an absentee ballot.

Laura looked at it closer.

"Donald J. Trump"

"Joseph R. Biden"

It was for this election. It was for right now. It hadn't been filled out. Laura remembered her mother asking her to send off for it, and somehow it had ended up in this pile. She kept looking at it. All she would have to do was mark it, and Joseph R. Biden would have another vote.

One last thing for her mother. Why not?

Her mother had been a lifelong Democrat. She'd always voted. She was still breathing, still a person of brain waves and heartbeats. In every way, she was a person legally alive, and if she could muster one more sentence, of course she would tell Laura to do this.

But what about the signature?

She looked again at her mother's stiffening arms and curling fingers. If only this had been two days before, when she could still lift her arms and move her hands.

"Go home," her sister told her. Rest. Tomorrow was going to be another long day.

"If she becomes lucid, get her to sign it," Laura said.

She put the ballot down and went home to bed, and that's where she was when her sister texted in the middle of the night—and while she had expected to cry when it happened, she hadn't expected to cry as hard as she was crying as she headed back to see her dead mother, thinking that whatever was left of her own life, and whatever it would turn out to mean, what would it mean without Meredith, what would it mean without Emily, what would it mean without Brent?

———

"FUCK," BRENT SAID a week later.

He was in the kitchen, starting to cook dinner, something he rarely did. It wasn't that he couldn't. In Jerusalem, he had cooked dinner for himself almost every night. A frozen chicken schnitzel, tossed into the oven. Frozen fries, tossed in next to the schnitzel. A pot of boiling water, some spaghetti, a jar of tomato sauce mixed in with ground-up lamb he got from the butcher in East Jerusalem, a nice man who seemed never to clean his knife but who Brent kept going to out of loyalty until he got sick with food poisoning and decided to find another butcher. Or chicken, from the new butcher, that he cooked outside on a grill. He was good on a grill, and he also knew how to deep-fry a turkey, which he did at home every Thanksgiving, and not once had a turkey caught fire and exploded. So he could do that, too.

But this was different. This was a meal kit that Laura had left for him before she flew out the door just after sunrise. She was still crying, though not nearly as much, and Brent really wanted this dinner to work out.

He looked at the instructions. "Bring a large pot of water to a boil for the potatoes."

"A large pot of water," he said, looking for a large pot, and meanwhile Laura was at one of the early voting centers, volunteering as a poll worker.

Her mother had done it for every election of Laura's childhood, and as Laura remembered it, there was such an uplifting innocence about it. The polling place was at the First Congregational Church, her mother would dress up a bit, and Laura would sit next to her, watching her check people in by flipping through an oversized ledger and looking for names. Laura had long wanted to do it, too, but there'd always been something in the way. Brent was in Iraq. Brent was in Israel. Brent was somewhere doing something, and someone had to meet Meredith's school bus. But now he was home, working in the dining room instead of downtown because of the pandemic, and Laura was experiencing something a world away from decades ago in Kansas.

There were police now at every location. And the rules—there were just so many, meant to ensure fairness but that in 2020 seemed like they would anger people who were increasingly suspicious. No phones in polling places. No cameras. No electronic devices of any kind. No guns, open-carry or concealed. No political T-shirts because that would be electioneering, so no Trump shirts, or Biden shirts either, although a Hillary shirt would be okay, even one that said HILLARY FOR PRISON, because she wasn't on the ballot. A Black Lives Matter shirt would be okay, too, and so would a Blue Lives Matter shirt, but not a MAGA shirt or a MAGA cap or a MAGA belt buckle or an uncovered MAGA tattoo. And no saying anything remotely political, not even "Tell her to take zinc. The president took it, and look at him," which was what one volunteer said to another whose friend had just tested positive for COVID. "Don't say the word 'president,'" he was told by a manager, who overheard him. "And you probably shouldn't say 'zinc' either." And one last rule, as things were about to get under way: "Be pleasant. Smile," the manager said to all of the volunteers, which meant that when someone showed up in a Trump T-shirt and was asked to take it off, and he refused, and he was asked again, and he refused again, poll workers kept suggesting alternatives until the man agreed to cover the word "Trump" in blue tape.

And if he hadn't agreed? If he had gotten angry? If he had started screaming? What would they have done?

"We had a firearm the other day," one of the workers said to another.

"Oh my gosh."

"It was just hanging out," he said, and the decision in that case was to just let the man be, let him vote, get him on his way.

It was all going so calmly. It all felt so on edge.

"Looks like a shredder," one voter said now to Laura of the voting machine she was standing next to.

His suspicious tone wasn't lost on her. "I *know*," she said, and then she went into the explanation she had been giving to every voter so they would have some faith in the system: "You're going to scan your ballot in there, and you'll wait a moment, and you'll hear a click, and once the counter goes up by one—see that counter there?—your vote is counted."

He slid his ballot into the feeder while Laura made a big show of looking away.

Click.

"There you go."

She pointed to the counter, which had gone up by one.

"Thank you and pick up a sticker on your way out," she said, and if a week ago she hadn't expected to cry so much about her mother, she hadn't expected to be enjoying this as much as she was. It was satisfying. It felt like she was doing something, and meanwhile, at home, Brent had found a big pot and was moving on to step two.

"Peel all potatoes and dice into one-inch pieces."

He wanted the dinner to be good for so many reasons, and one was that when Laura's mother had died, he'd been away at another event with Finn. He'd told her he didn't think he should go away, but she'd insisted, saying it could be days, so he'd gone, and while she was dealing with a funeral home, he was in a field in Mississippi, talking to another dog owner and hearing a story that a few days later was still bothering him.

The man told Brent he had gone to Arkansas to duck-hunt on a river with his nine-year-old grandson. The rules were that no boats could be put in the water before eight A.M., but that applied only to public access, the man said. He had access to the water through private land, and by sunup he and his grandson were out on the river putting out duck decoys.

And that was when another boat came barreling toward them, the man said. There were two men in it, one was yelling something about cheating, and the boat kept coming and coming and rammed into his, almost sending his grandson into the water.

"And I lost it," the man said. "I picked up my oar, and I smashed that motherfucker in the head."

That might have been the end of it, the man said. The other boat left. The boy, he said, seemed okay, and they went back to putting out decoys from their dented boat. But a while later came the sound of another boat.

"Are they coming back?" he said the boy asked him.

"No," the man said as the boat closed in on them, seeing the two wildlife officers.

"Now here's what's going to happen," he told his grandson. "They're going to want to talk to us. They're going to want to talk to you. And I want you to be honest. Tell them what happened. Tell them the boat rammed us. You almost fell in. I was angry. I picked up an oar and swung it. I hit a man. They may come onto our boat. They may ask us to follow them to the dock. When we get there, they're probably going to take me to jail, and you'll have to go with some people you don't know, but it'll be okay. You'll have a good lunch, and then I'll come get you."

Then he was talking to the officer.

"My only regret is I didn't hit him with my metal paddle," he said.

Brent and the man were standing in the shade of a tree as the man finished his story, and part of him was appalled, and part of him admired the man's honesty. But the thing that was sticking with him days later was one other thing the man said he had told his grandson, just after he had swung the oar and felt it smash into the man's head.

"That rage is in all of us," he said to his grandson. "It's in me, and it's in you, too."

All of us, he had said, and that was the part Brent couldn't shake. Was it in everyone?

"All of us?" Brent said now as he finished the potatos.

He shook his head and looked at the instructions. "Okay, dice the apples into one-inch pieces," he said, moving on, as some pieces of potato dropped to the floor and both Finn and Sampson made beelines for them.

"Balsamic vinegar?" he said, looking at the next step, shaking his head again. "It's not like she picked the easiest recipe."

His phone lit up. It was a message from Laura. The polls were closed. She'd be leaving soon.

"It's not like I'm making Hamburger Helper here," Brent said. "All right. Water's boiling."

He dumped the potatoes into the water. Hot water splashed onto the stove.

"Hey!" he yelled at the dogs as they made another run at the potatoes on the floor.

"In a large pot or Dutch oven, heat one to two tablespoons of oil," he said, reading the next step, and then he read it again. "In a large pot or Dutch oven . . ." The large pot had potatoes in it, so where was the Dutch oven? There it was, in the sink, dirty from yesterday when Laura had fried some pickles in it. And where was the oil? He checked every cabinet. He couldn't find the oil.

"This could all come to a crashing halt," he said. "I don't know what I'm going to do."

He kept staring at the directions.

"Butter!" he said. "I'm going to use butter."

He cleaned the Dutch oven. He melted some butter. He grabbed the chicken to brown it. Some of the raw juice spilled onto the counter and he cleaned it with Windex. He heard the garage door opening.

"Crap. She's home."

He turned to Meredith, who had been watching all of this. "Mer, did you see the orchid I bought Mom?" he asked her, and when she didn't say anything, he said, "How about giving her a hug? Make her feel good?"

"Hi, Mer!" Laura said, walking in. "How are you? You making dinner? You helping Dad?"

"Hey," Brent said to her. "This is a pretty complicated meal."

She looked at the pots on the stove, the potato bits on the floor, the Windex.

"Why didn't you just go get Mexican?" she asked.

Brent hung his head. "Why didn't I get Mexican?" he said to himself.

Too late now.

"Chop dill."

He chopped dill.

"Mash to desired consistency."

He mashed to desired consistency.

"Scoop sweet potato mash onto a plate and then top with chicken, apples, and sauce."

Almost done.

"Okay," he said. "Add salt and pepper."

What a train wreck.

"Laura?" he yelled, not sure where she had gone.

"Yup?" she yelled back.

"It's ready."

He put the plate in front of her, next to the orchid. She took a bite, and the look on her face was one to remember.

"Mmm," she said, smiling.

She reached for another bite. "I *like* this."

THAT SMILE—THAT was the life promised.

The dog he was now watching swim at sunup across Lake Lanier—that was it, too.

"Good dog! *Good* dog! Good swim. That's a good boy."

The beer on his porch at sunset. The grass growing in the backyard where the trampoline used to be. Meredith, eating fresh orange slices with such pleasure and lining up the peels along the rim of her plate with such precision, his artist.

All of his life. All of it.

So why, as the election got closer, did it feel increasingly flimsy?

"Colonel Cummings?" someone was saying now.

He was at a pharmacy, handing over an empty pill bottle to get a refill and looking in sudden bewilderment at the person working behind the counter. He seemed young, but it was hard to tell. Most of his face was covered by a mask because of the pandemic. Brent had no idea who this person was.

Sensing confusion, he reminded Brent of his name—Nick—and then called him "sir," and the "sir" was what jogged something loose.

He had been a cadet. Brent was pretty sure of it. More than that he couldn't remember, but that was enough for him to tell Nick it was good to see him again, and meanwhile Nick, bewildered, too, by such a chance meeting, was suddenly replaying one of the most transformative moments of his life.

It had happened on a day he'd reported to Brent's office, in all probability to be dropped from the program because of the way he had been behaving.

"Knock three times," he was instructed as he stood on one side of the bad door.

"Report," Brent had hollered from the other side, wondering what knucklehead was about to walk through.

In all of his time as a cadet, Nick had never met with Brent one-on-one, and he was so anxious about it that two days before the meeting he had texted one of the upperclassmen who supervised him.

"Sir," he had texted, "could you help me with something before my meeting with COL Cummings on Thursday?"

"Depends on what it is," was the answer.

"A piece of writing helping me to make my case for not getting dropped?"

"I cannot do this," came the reply.

Three hours later, near midnight, Nick texted him again. "Does that mean I'm most likely getting dropped or not sir? I'm very nervous about all of this, I'm sorry to bother you about it."

"I wish I had an answer for you on that. Unfortunately I don't. It's fully out of my hands. You can't worry yourself this much."

"Yes sir, I'll try not to worry so much. I'll have an answer on Thursday after my meeting with the COL at 1530," Nick had written back, but as he walked into Brent's office, he was so worried and nervous he felt like he might pass out.

He saluted and stood at parade rest while Brent looked through the paperwork he had been given. A four-year scholarship recipient. A biochemistry major. Missing classes. Poor attitude.

"Why are you doing the things you're doing?" he

asked Nick, and as Nick would remember it later, that was the start of his transformation.

"I could have explained to him why I was such a shit-head," was how he would describe it. He'd never explained it to anyone. Now he had the opportunity, and as Brent told him to take a seat, he wondered whether he should.

"I was praying that he would have a little, I don't know, is mercy the right word?" he said. "Grace?"

NINE YEARS BEFORE THAT, when Nick was twelve years old, he was sitting at a table with his mother, listening to the plan she had come up with so he never would have to see his father again. It involved breaking one of his fingers and saying his father had done it. She put a hammer on the table.

"Are you going to hit me?" he would remember asking her.

"No," he would remember her saying. "You are."

So he picked up the hammer and brought it down on one of his fingers.

It was November 2009, and his parents were in the depths of a custody battle that would end up in court again and again, culminating in Nick's mother, Karen, pleading guilty to charges of aggravated stalking and contributing to the delinquency of a minor. "Judge," the lawyer representing her that day said, "this has been a, quite frankly, God-awful custody dispute for the past decade . . . lots of allegations began floating around all over the place about abuse this, abuse that, and to make a long story short, Karen got in the middle of it and did some things she shouldn't have done, bottom line. And that's why she's standing here pleading guilty."

That testimony was in one of the many court files that accumulated over the years, eight in all, two criminal and six civil, one of which contained a psychological evaluation of Nick's mother in which she described what Nick had been like before all of this, "that Nick has been in gifted classes since kindergarten and that his grades are usually A's and B's. She added that Nick is also athletic and very sociable."

By the time 2009 rolled around, his parents had been divorced for nine years, and Nick saw his father only sporadically, even though he lived close by. There had been back-and-forth accusations and denials between his parents of drug use and domestic violence during their marriage. Nick's mother also had said that after their divorce, Nick's father had had sex with a woman in a motel while Nick was in the next bed—"There is no indication that this happened," a judge said—that he had "pornography in the home"—"There is no evidence to support this whatsoever"—and that he had driven drunk with Nick in his car—"There was no evidence to support this allegation."

Dismissing the idea that Nick's father "would decapitate and disembowel Nicholas" if he were to stay at his father's, the judge ordered regular visits to resume. That was in September 2009, and two months later, during one of those visits, things escalated from contentious into what his mother's lawyer would describe at her sentencing as "just an all-around horrible situation."

It began when Nick texted his mother to say that unlike in previous visits, his father had allowed him to keep his phone close by. "i didnt let him take it this time," he texted.

"good 4u," his mother texted back, adding that "if u need 2 fight" him, she was home and he could come there.

"alright," Nick texted back.

"u should distract the hell out of him," she texted.

"how so?" he asked.

"make sum noise. party!"

"yeaaaaaaaa! haha i will"

"do sumthin repeatative 2 anoy him then tell him 2 fucj off til he gets mad then laugh @ him," she wrote, and a minute later added, "drums bang bang bang"

"haha," Nick wrote back.

"b obnoxious"

"want me to run? i can," he wrote a little later, and when she didn't reply, he wrote, "seriously mom i need an answer . . . i could be home in 2 seconds"

"did he do sumthin," she wrote back.

"no but i wanna be home," he wrote back.

"cum on," she wrote, so he ran home to his mother— and to the hammer.

He chose his ring finger on his left hand. He was scared, and it took him a while, but eventually he gathered his courage and swung.

It wasn't hard enough to break a bone.

Try again, he would remember his mother saying. He did, but after two more tries he couldn't do it anymore. She picked up the hammer, but she couldn't do it either, so instead she called the police to report that her son had been injured by his father, and when they didn't seem terribly interested, she took Nick to the emergency room, where he said the injury had happened when his father tried to twist his phone out of his hand. An examination showed swelling but "no evidence of underlying fracture or dislocation," and he was sent home.

Two weeks later, when he was at his father's again, his mother came up with a new plan.

"She told me she had hidden a baseball bat in the bushes outside of his house. She wanted me to hit him in his head," was how he would describe it, years later. "She didn't want me to kill him, she wanted something to tell the court, that 'He was doing something so bad, my son had to hit him.'"

The texts that day began when she coached him on what to say to the police.

"if cops ask he keeps tryin 2 take ur new fone away & its 3rd 1 moms bought u & u keep it in ur underwear & he keeps tryin 2 get it outa ur pants. tell em its not ok w u 4 him 2 touch u dwn there & ur not gona let him touch u again wo defendin urself."

She also told him that if he found "anything like porn hide it outside" and "look 4 camers in the house 1st"

"Alright ill hide the stuff in the left bushes," he texted back.

"jus let me no when its there & when i can cum get it," she wrote.

"K," he wrote. "hey if i kick his knee in and break it will i go to juvy"

"not if u say what i jus told u 2 say that hes tryin 2 get ur fone outa ur underwear & hes not gona touch u there anymore!"

Then she sent a few more messages:

"say he grabbed a handful of ur hair & jerked ur neck. scalp tender. bite him if u ev get a chance"

"make sure u erase"

"do what u thinks best! i trust ur judgement. if u cant its ok. dont feel u have 2 nick."

Then, as Nick would describe it years later:

"I hit him with the bat."

It was a full-sized wooden bat. Nick found it in the bushes, took it inside the house and waited, and when his father walked into the kitchen, he swung it into his father's forehead.

"I didn't hit him that hard," Nick would say, although photographs in the court file show a man bleeding from a gash above his right eye, with more blood dripping down his right cheek and more on the floor.

"My plan was to hit him and run back to my mother," he would say, but his father tackled him and called the police.

"He was holding Nick down so that Nick would not run away or do any other destructive acts," was how a judge described those initial moments, after hearing a 911 recording. He also noted that Nick's father's voice was "very calm under the circumstances on the 911 tape even though Nick is screaming bloody murder."

More precisely, he was a twelve-year-old boy who was screaming bloody murder, a boy who had been told to break his own finger with a hammer and to hit his father with a baseball bat, and what started his long road back to stability was his father's decision not to press charges. Instead, while his mother went to jail and was then put on probation, Nick moved in with his father.

He graduated from high school. He got a four-year ROTC scholarship to the University of North Georgia. He turned eighteen. He seemed to be doing well, but he was also developing an attitude. "A punk" was how he would describe what he was becoming. He was being especially disrespectful to women, and while that might have been understandable because of what his mother had done to him, something that once understood could be remedied, he didn't give it a second thought. He was so lacking in self-reflection and empathy that when he casually said to his father one day, "Hey, sorry about that bat thing," and his father, tearing up, grateful for the words, said, "I know it's not your fault," the weight of those forgiving words didn't even register. "I already knew that," he thought to himself.

As for what had happened with the hammer, he had never said a word about it to anyone. No one knew.

And then came a message one day saying that Brent wanted to see him.

"And I'm scared out of my mind," Nick would say. "He's the guy you don't ever want to be one-on-one with."

Whatever was going to happen, he was hoping it would go quickly, and when Brent asked him his first question—"Why are you doing what you're doing?"— Nick decided he would be honest. No excuses. That was going to be his strategy.

"I made mistakes, sir," he said. "I take full responsibility. Moving forward, this kind of thing is not going to happen again."

Here came his punishment. He readied himself.

"Take a seat," Brent said.

He wasn't expecting that.

"Nick, what is it that you want to do in the Army?"

He wasn't expecting that, either. Be honest, he reminded himself, so he told Brent his plan to join the medical services branch of the Army after graduating, and if he were ever deployed to a war zone, to save some lives.

"And then he said to me that when he was downrange, the type of person I was? He would not want that kind of person to be responsible for his life," Nick would remember of what Brent said to him.

There was his mercy. That sentence.

"It was the first time an adult ever said to me, 'I expect more of you,'" Nick said. "It made me question my entire existence. I was: 'I want to save lives.' And he was: 'You? Get away from me.'"

He could have said something about the hammer then. He could have said something about the bat, his mother, all of it. His chance to explain the shithead he had become had arrived. Instead, he sat in silence, burning with shame.

There was his grace. That shame.

"Because he shamed me to make me right," Nick said.

YEARS BEFORE, just after Meredith had been born, in his own moment of shame, Brent had listened as his father said, "You're going to love her."

Did his father ever know how much those words meant? Eighteen years had passed since his father had said them. Eleven years had passed since he'd died. And Brent was hearing them still. They had stung him initially, and since then they had guided him into the man he had become, all the way to this moment of handing over an empty pill bottle to someone who had left Brent's office that day, began taking himself more seriously, became kinder, became more compassionate, stayed in the program, graduated, and was waiting to hear what graduate school was going to accept him into its medical program.

The long, mattering trails of a life—and Brent had no idea.

"It's good to see you, sir," Nick said, and Brent said likewise and hurried off, glad he was getting cholesterol medication this day and nothing more awkward. He went home, back to his porch, back to his questions about purpose and meaning, back to his Twitter feed. Election Day was close now, and had the Twitter version of America ever been more noxious?

"Hey, Colonel," Michael called from his driveway.

"Hey," he called back from his porch, continuing to scroll. "Strange times," he said.

"Sir?" Michael said.

"Strange times," Brent said again, louder.

"Yes, sir," Michael said. "Strange times. All we can do is just pray to the good Lord. He's in control."

"Yeah," Brent said.

"I know we're not," Michael said.

"Yeah," Brent said.

A low-flying plane drowned out whatever Michael said next, and after it had passed, he said, "Well, I'm going to go into the house."

It was all so polite, as if their earlier, tense conversation hadn't happened, and once again Brent found himself wondering about what that man had said that day about rage. Was rage in Michael? He certainly had reason to feel cheated about life, but Brent had never seen Michael act in any way other than neighborly. Even in their earlier conversation, Michael hadn't so much as raised his voice, but if he had gotten angry that day, anger wasn't what that man had been talking about. It was destructive anger, anger out of control, resulting in a certain kind of action. An oar, swung. There was no way Michael had that in him, and when he thought about it more broadly, measuring the U.S. against what he had seen in other parts of the world, he didn't think Americans were a rageful people. Some were, but most wanted no part of it. He was sure of it.

He went back to scrolling through tweets. The closer Election Day got, the more he couldn't keep away.

"JUST VOTED," Trump tweeted on October 24, with ten days to go. "A great honor!"

"I don't think it's a good idea to wait till Election Day," Laura said to Brent. "I say go early. I say go now. You don't know what's going to happen."

"Well thank you for the advice," Brent said, "but I want to vote on Election Day."

October 27 now. "7 DAYS!!!" Trump tweeted.

October 30. "This election is the most important election of our lifetime! Get out and VOTE to #MAGA!"

October 31. "There is only one way to defend your dignity. There is only one way to defend your family and your Country. There is only one way to preserve, protect and defend the American Way of Life: you must show up and vote on November 3rd!"

November 1. Two days to go. "Joe Biden is the candidate of rioters, looters, arsonists, gun-grabbers, flag-burners, Marxists, lobbyists, and special interests. I am the candidate of farmers, factory workers, police officers, and hard-working, law-abiding patriots of every race, religion and creed!"

November 2 now. "MAKE AMERICA GREAT AGAIN!" Trump tweeted, and meanwhile, Laura was bringing Brent a slice of birthday cake.

"I didn't realize till Sunday that there's a difference between white frosting and vanilla frosting," she said, and asked him: "Which do you like?"

"Vanilla," he said.

"Well, this is white," she said.

He took a bite.

"Yeah," he said, "I like vanilla."

That night, before bed, he took stock of his life. He was an ordinary man. That's who he had become. He was fifty-two years old, special to some, unknown to most, a bit of a dreamer, and not just that bad dream. He had others. But he was also a realist. He had wanted to change the world, but he wasn't going to do that. Because what can an ordinary man do?

He slept fitfully, and when he woke up it was Election Day, and the president was at it again, tweeting away:

"VOTE! VOTE! VOTE!"

CHAPTER 10

BY SIX A.M., the first person was in line, even though sunrise was an hour away.

By six-thirty, a sheriff's deputy was circling the parking lot, just in case.

At seven sharp, someone was unlocking the doors and announcing, "Okay, polls are open," and at seven-fifteen, Michael was pulling up in his van.

"Let me put a mask on so they don't throw me out," he said.

Mask on. Bungee cord off. Ramp down, and soon he was inside filling out his ballot, and then headed back home, where in the house next door, Brent was calling out, "Hey, I'm going to vote."

"Here to vote?" a volunteer asked Brent a few minutes later.

"Yes, sir," he said, and soon he was filling out his ballot and feeding it into the scanner. There came the click as it registered and the counter went up by one, and then he had headed home, where in the house next door, Michael was saying, "I don't know, but I still think Trump is going to win."

"We shall see what happens," Brent said, inside his own house.

"My heart of hearts, we're going to wake up tomorrow, and there will have been such a big red wave it will be indisputable," Michael said.

"I want the landslide victory tonight because it affirms the way we ought to be," Brent said.

"Voting for freedom or voting for socialism," Michael said of the choice. "Even if they do win, I'll be fucked if I'm going to let that happen."

"I want to believe in the fundamental goodness of people," Brent said.

That night, when Laura got home, he said to her, "I don't know. I'm not very confident right now."

"Neither am I," Laura said.

The next morning, he felt worse as he read what Trump had said overnight when there were the first indications that if he lost, he wouldn't concede: "This is a fraud on the American public. This is an embarrassment to our country. We were getting ready to win this election. Frankly we did win this election . . ."

"This is disgusting," Brent said. "This is un-American."

The next day, as Biden moved closer to having enough electoral votes to have won, Trump spoke again. "If you count the legal votes, I easily win. If you count the illegal votes, they can try to steal the election from us," he began.

"Sick," Brent said.

The next day, it was Biden's turn to speak. He had enough electoral votes now to be the president-elect, and although Congress still had to go through the formality of approving the results, it was over, at least according to these counts. Here it was, then, Brent's moment of relief, and of affirmation, especially when Biden said: "I've always believed we can define America in one word: possibilities. That in America everyone should be given the opportunity to go as far as their dreams and God-given ability will take them. You see, I believe in the possibility of this country."

His president-elect was saying exactly what Brent had been told to believe. It was what his father had promised him, and what he in turn had promised, too, to Emily, to Meredith, to the students he had once counseled, and to his soldiers when they had come to him banged-up and disillusioned.

And yet he didn't believe it, not in this moment. No matter what Biden said, it wasn't over because it wasn't Biden's words he was hearing, it was Trump's, and now Trump was speaking again:

"We fight. We fight like hell," he was saying. "And if you don't fight like hell, you're not going to have a country anymore."

It was January 6. The only thing left was for Congress to certify the vote, at which point Trump would officially be the loser.

"Fight for Trump," people were chanting.

"We love Trump," they chanted.

"We love you."

"So," Trump said to a crowd that included people

with knives, bats, chemical spray, brass knuckles, Tasers, zip-ties, the makings of a gallows, batons, and Trump flags on poles they soon would be smashing into police officers trying to keep them out of the Capitol, "let's walk down Pennsylvania Avenue."

The crowd began to move, and as Trump watched for a moment, it was impossible for anyone who wasn't him to know what he was thinking. He seemed joyless. He wasn't smiling, as he did sometimes when crowds told him they loved him. And he certainly wasn't laughing because he never laughed, not publicly, except for one time during a campaign rally when he was talking about immigration and border crossings.

"How do you stop these people?" he had said. "You can't."

"Shoot them!" someone had yelled.

That was what he had laughed at, and Brent had realized he knew that laughter. He had been dreaming about it for years.

WHEN BRENT WAS six years old, he was on his grandfather's farm in Mississippi, walking around with a pellet rifle, when he spotted a toad in a puddle of water and fired three times.

Three shots, three hits, all close together into the back of the head from the dead-eye aim of a six-year-old boy. The pride Brent felt was because he was from a family of hunters, and now he was one of them. He called to his grandfather and his uncle to come see what he had done, and all these years later, he was still hearing what his uncle said.

"Why would you do that?"

Without saying another word, his grandfather and uncle walked away. Only when they were gone did he pick the toad out of the water and toss it into some weeds where no one could see it, and with that, shame entered his soul for the first time and was still there thirty-three years later when his life brought him to a hopeless town in Iraq called Kamaliyah.

It was April 2007, early in the deployment, and Brent was still believing in the mission even though he was staring down at that body floating in that septic tank in that factory on the edge of town.

"Headless, toeless, fingerless," said the soldier Brent was with, a captain who was in charge of a company of one hundred twenty soldiers, all of whom were supposed to move into that building.

"Well, what I think we do is," Brent said and trailed off. "Man." He had no idea what to do. But it needed to be done because that was part of the mission. Soldiers were supposed to live in towns rather than faraway bases. That would make the people feel safer. If the people felt safer, they would turn against the insurgents. If the insurgents were gone, the war would be over. Win the people, win the war, that was the idea, and Brent believed in it, which was why he had to get that body out of the septic tank.

"I mean someone has disgraced him as bad as you can possibly disgrace a human being," Brent said. "And there's not a playbook that we can go to that says when you open it up: 'Here's how you remove a body from a septic tank.'"

It was as absurd a conversation as a war could ask for, and in the end, one that wouldn't even matter because the insurgents had figured out what the Americans had in mind. Before the soldiers could move in, the building was packed one night with explosives and blown up. And yet right up to that moment, Brent continued to treat a corpse adrift in water not as an absurdity but as a moral imperative. "I mean, he was somebody's son, and maybe husband, and for dignity's sake, well, it cheapens us to leave him there," he said of why he was trying so hard to come up with a solution. "I would hope someone would do the same for my body. And for any human being."

That was what the war was for him in those early days, the chance to do things right.

"Otherwise, we're not human," he said. It was one of the finest moments of his life.

And then came the last days.

It was a year later, bombs were going off everywhere, every convoy was being shot at, roads were lined with burning tires, and the skies were filling with smoke.

"Fucking assholes. Fucking asshole," Brent kept saying.

Win the people, win the war.

It was out of control, and it was all a surprise because for the last several weeks everything had been calm. The soldiers were just about done with the deployment. They had started packing to go home. Two weeks to go, that was all, that was what they were down to, and then an

Iraqi cleric named Muqtada al-Sadr, one of the most powerful people in Iraq, called for an all-out attack on U.S. forces, and for the first time Brent was seeing what one person with enormous power over obeying masses could unleash.

"Our worst nightmare is coming true," Brent said at one point, on March 26, 2008, as he monitored radio transmissions that were at times difficult to hear because of all the gunfire.

March 27 now. Mortars. Rockets. Rocket-propelled grenades. Everything.

March 28 now. As the soldiers tried to sleep, back in the U.S. Donald Trump was announcing the newest winner of his TV show *Celebrity Apprentice*. "You're a vicious guy," Trump was saying to the winner and a viewing audience of twelve million people, his way of offering congratulations.

March 29 now. Was that faint noise a boom?

Another second or two went by, and then someone was on the radio, screaming. One vehicle destroyed. Soldiers in need of evacuation. A few minutes passed. The radio was filled with the sound of gunfire. A few more minutes passed. The phone was ringing and someone was handing the receiver to Brent's commander.

"All right, buddy. Hang in there. Standing by," he said and hung up.

"What'd he say, sir?" Brent asked.

"Two KIA," he said, his eyes filling with tears.

Brent's were too, and it wasn't long after that, when the monitors showed an insurgent coming around the corner of a building and blasting away at a convoy, un-

aware of the remote camera locked in on him, and that he
was about to be shot into too many pieces to count, that
Brent began to yell, "Die, monkey, die."

Around the room, heads turned.

"Die, monkey, die," he yelled again, and now others
joined in. Aieti, who was already dreaming of that burning soldier. Prestley, who soon would be going home to
his wife and two daughters in Kansas. There were a dozen
people in the room and they were all chanting now, led by
Brent, who, suddenly hearing himself, stopped.

He had never felt more ashamed.

"Fight over. Congratulations again on a job well done.
I'm really proud of you," his father wrote to him a few
days later as his war came to an end, and soon he was
home, and soon after that he was having his dream. The
first time left him gasping for breath. The second time, he
understood it would come a third time, and a fourth, and
it had, hundreds of times since, always the same blackness, always the same laughter at his naïveté, right up to
January 6, 2020, when he was once again witnessing what
one person with enormous power could unleash.

All along he had been thinking he had left war behind,
but as he watched the mob swarming the Capitol, it occurred to him that he *had* been naïve. Americans did understand violence, so he had been wrong about that.
They were capable of rage, so he had been wrong about
that, too. And his war wasn't over. It was just that it was
here now, not there, and the enemy was no longer them.
It was becoming the American next door.

His neighbor, Michael.

Michael's neighbor. Him.

Anyone's neighbor.

Rage over what was happening felt like it was everywhere now. In Brent, too. The accusations about voter fraud. The lying. The relentlessness of it. The shamelessness of it. Ever since Election Day, when he had walked out of the voting booth with the belief that his vote would matter, and then had watched helplessly as people tried to warp his vote, to undermine it and turn it into something worthless, a sense of growing outrage had been building in him, and when he saw Michael outside one day—Michael who believed that Trump had won, that the corrupt Democrats had been secretly planning and plotting what was happening for years, that it was left-wing radicals such as Antifa who had stormed the Capitol, that if Biden were declared the winner he would soon be revealed as senile and replaced by socialists and communists; Michael whose own outrage had been building—Brent went over to see him.

"Good morning! How are you?" Michael called, watching him approach.

The houses were only a few feet apart, and yet in the span of those few feet was an American landscape that felt as wide as the entire country.

"How are you?" Brent said, on Michael's driveway now.

"My right leg is quite swollen compared to my left," Michael said.

"Yeah?" Brent said.

"So I have to get that looked at," Michael said. "It's heavier, too."

"Huh," Brent said.

"I don't know what that's about," Michael said. "With paralysis, it could be a blood clot, it could be nothing. You know?"

"Yeah," Brent said.

"I've had three Doppler studies on this leg over the past twelve years looking for blood clots but they found nothing. Just could be the way it is," Michael said.

"Yeah," Brent said. "How many years has it been now since you got injured?"

"Thirty," Michael said.

"Wow," Brent said.

"Twenty-nine plus," Michael said.

Everything about the moment felt jittery, including the air itself, which was filled with sounds of sirens.

"I don't know what's going on," Brent said. "There have been all kinds of fire trucks, ambulances—"

"I heard it myself," Michael said. "I wonder what it's all about."

"I don't see any smoke anywhere," Brent said. "I hope it isn't something . . ." He trailed off.

"Yeah, that's always scary," Michael said.

"Yeah," Brent said.

They both fell silent, and Michael went back to what he had been doing before Brent came over, loading some things in his van. He was struggling.

Brent watched. Then he said, "Can I help?"

And for the next few minutes, that was what he did. He helped.

"Thank you, Colonel," Michael said when they had finished. "Thank you very much."

"No problem," Brent said, heading back to his house.

Everything still felt jittery to him, but not as jittery. The distance between the houses still felt wide to him, but not as wide. "You're going to love her," his father had said. And he had.

Was that what it took?

FOUR MONTHS LATER, he woke up before sunup, got dressed, brushed his teeth, combed his hair, and took a quick look at himself in the mirror.

"Are you okay?" Laura asked him.

"Why wouldn't I be?" was what he wanted to say.

"Yeah," was what he did say.

He fed Finn and said he was going for a drive.

"You okay?" Laura asked again.

He kissed her, loaded Finn into his truck, loaded in one of his shotguns, drove out of Pleasantville, and headed west.

It was Memorial Day, a day that had gotten increasingly mournful for him in the years since Iraq. He supposed he should go to a public ceremony of some kind, or a military cemetery, but instead he got a cup of coffee and kept driving until he was in a part of Georgia that was deep in the heart of Donald Trump territory. There were still Trump signs in yards and nailed to trees, and he guessed they would be there forever.

It wasn't lost on him that one of the things he despised about Trump was his lack of empathy, and here he was, incapable of anything kinder. But every day since Election Day had done that to him, and Trump's behavior on January 20, Inauguration Day, had cemented it in. "It's

going to happen" was how Brent had started that final
day of Trump's presidency, and then, giving in to the un-
certainties Trump had created, he'd amended that. "Is it
going to happen?" With less than four hours to go until
noon, when the Twentieth Amendment dictates a new
presidential term begins, he was still wondering as he'd
watched Trump get on *Marine One* and fly away from a
city where, because of him, there were twenty-five thousand National Guard troops to help keep peace. He had
listened, nodding, to what was being said on TV: "Repre-
hensible" . . . "Grievances and lies" . . . "He is leaving in
disgrace." He had watched as Trump, after landing at
Joint Base Andrews, spoke his final words as president,
"So have a good life, we will see you soon, thank you,
thank you very much," and the fact that Trump then got
on a plane to fly away, rather than attend the inauguration, was what had gotten to Brent most of all. It was the
final act of a coward. "Good riddance," he had said as
Trump waved and boarded Air Force One, and at 11:59
A.M., unable to sit for another moment, standing now,
leaning forward, eyes glued to the TV, willing it to happen, he'd said, "One minute, one minute," and then it
was noon and President Joseph R. Biden was saying, "We
must meet this moment as the *United* States of America,"
and Brent was turning away from the TV to Laura.
"Wow," he had said, and then had said quieter, to himself, not so much about Biden but about the country,
"Good wins."

Four months later, the sun was up now. He had always
loved being outside in this light, the first light, when the
feeling of a day's promise was at its purest, and he wanted

to take it fully in. The morning was still chilly. The windows were up. He turned on the radio. He kept driving, through towns and pine stands. His thoughts at that point were still drifting. His mood at that point was contentment.

An hour or so after leaving home, he reached the base of Garland Mountain and began driving up. At the top was a sporting-clays facility where he could practice his shooting, and on this Memorial Day, that was where he wanted to be. Just him, by himself, and his Beretta 694 shotgun, and whatever thoughts came to mind.

The facility wasn't open yet when he got there, but someone was at the desk, and he was able to sign in and say he wanted to shoot one hundred rounds. He was hungry, but the restaurant wasn't open yet either. A waitress, early for her shift, brought him a cup of coffee, and he sat by himself at a table, listening to the conversations as a few more people came in.

"Beautiful day."

"Yes, it is."

"Absolutely beautiful."

And it was. It was absolutely beautiful.

Here came the waitress again to take his order, and here came his pancakes, and here came his bacon, and here came three more customers, a man about his age, his son, probably, and his father, probably, and here came thoughts of his own father and his first tears of the day.

He was glad he was sitting by himself and that no one could see him.

He wiped his eyes. He pulled himself together. He finished his pancakes.

Here came the waitress, looking over her shoulder for some reason as she approached, and saying very quietly to him, "Are you a veteran?"

"Yeah," he said. "I am."

She had already placed his check on the table, and now she picked it up, began walking away, turned back, and pointed at him.

"I want to make sure I give you a discount," she said.

"Okay," he said, and after she was out of sight, he began laughing.

This was what those fourteen soldiers had died for?

A ten percent discount?

His thoughts were no longer drifting.

"Thank you," he said when she came back, and he paid the bill and then went outside into the beautiful day.

His first shot couldn't have been better. He hit the flying clay dead on, and it exploded into several pieces. His second shot was just as true, and his third. A great shot anyway, he was really on his game today. A fourth shot.

Perfect.

A fifth.

And on it went until feelings of guilt began creeping in and he began missing.

It was guilt over the pleasure he was feeling.

"Look, man, it's not your fault," he told himself.

Guilt over how well he was shooting.

"You gotta live life."

Over being alive on a beautiful day.

"Shoot the clay."

So he shot the clay, hitting some and missing some, and more thoughts kept coming at him, as he'd known they would since he awakened. The physically dead, the mentally dead, the physically injured, the mentally injured, the morally injured, all of them, even himself— and for what? What were their sacrifices for? Was it all so someone could come along a decade later and get elected president and try to divide the United States into a broken country that would produce even more people ruined by war?

"Enjoy the view," he told himself, and he tried, but it was too late.

He was in his truck now, driving down the mountain as if he were being chased. Here was his dream at last, on him in full force, not during the night when he had come to expect it and was learning how to fight it off, but in daylight, in his truck, windows down, air rushing in. Here was the dream, and he screamed.

It was a scream unlike any in his life. He screamed again and slammed the steering wheel. "It's going to be all right, it's going to be all right," he told himself, trying to get under control, but then he screamed again, and he kept screaming all the way down the mountain.

He was crying now. For thirteen years, he had been trying every day to recover from the man he had become in war to the man he wanted to be in peace, and where had he gotten in that effort? He wasn't a better man, not yet, only a man who still wanted to be better and suddenly wished to be home. He stopped crying. He stopped screaming. He hit the gas. He headed east. It took him an hour, but then he was pulling up to his house, and this time when Laura asked, "Are you okay?" his answer was, "I'm good."

In fracturing America, he grilled some hamburgers, drank a beer, sat for a while on his porch, and headed to bed that night, hoping. Sooner or later, the dream would return. It would mock him. It would terrify him. He knew it was coming. But for now he was still believing in the possibilities of his promised country, and clinging to them, including the possibility that even in America some dreams never come true.

ACKNOWLEDGMENTS

The first acknowledgment needs to be to the people who agreed to be in this book. Even in the best of times, it takes a certain courage to have the intimacies of a life written about, and as the people in the book make clear, these are not the best of times. For that reason alone, I want to acknowledge those who weighed the advantages of remaining private and decided instead that in a civilized world, true stories need to be told and heard.

In addition, I'd like to thank the following people:

Kate Medina, for brilliant editing and her reassuring belief that allowed me to find this book.

Melanie Jackson, for, among other things, our many years of many conversations.

At Random House: Andy Ward, Rachel Rokicki, London King, Ayelet Durantt, Dennis Ambrose, Benjamin Dreyer, Monica Brown for her kindness and patience, and Matthew Martin for having the mind of a lawyer and the heart of a reader.

In Georgia: Addyson Albershardt and Amber Massey.

In Iraq: the soldiers of the 2-16 and, in particular, Ralph Kauzlarich, for whom there can never be enough thanks.

In Israel: Eli Matityahu and his welcoming family; Mary Fitzgerald.

At *The Washington Post:* Don Graham, Leonard Downie, Jr., Bob Thompson, Bill Hamilton, Kevin Merida, Marcus Brauchli, Liz Spayd, Marty Baron, Sally Buzbee, Cameron Barr, Steven Ginsberg, Matea Gold, Phil Rucker, Jill Grisco, and Katharine Weymouth.

The John D. and Catherine T. MacArthur Foundation.

The American Presidency Project at the University of California, Santa Barbara.

Andon Prestley, for her compassion and inspiring honesty.

David Klein, Eric Estrin, and Tom Shroder for getting me started and for that dinner.

Bob Barnes, Lynne Perri, Tim Hester, Francie Hester, Lucian Perkins, Sarah Tanguy, Steve Adler, Steve Coll, Dana Priest, Anne Hull, and Peter Perl for their sustaining friendships.

Phil Bennett, Stephanie McCrummen, Eli Saslow, and Katherine Boo for their own work and for urging this book into life.

My family: Julia Post, Lauren Lewis, Jonathan Post, and Adam Lewis for their love and encouragement; Olivia Post, Elizabeth Lewis, Evelyn Post, Lincoln Lewis, and Andrew Post for their love and distractions; and Lisa Hill for all of the artistry that has come after that magical word "okay."

ABOUT THE AUTHOR

DAVID FINKEL is a journalist and author whose honors include a Pulitzer Prize and a MacArthur Foundation "Genius" grant. A writer and editor at *The Washington Post*, he lives in the Washington, D.C., area.

ABOUT THE TYPE

This book was set in Sabon, a typeface designed by the well-known German typographer Jan Tschichold (1902–74). Sabon's design is based upon the original letter forms of sixteenth-century French type designer Claude Garamond and was created specifically to be used for three sources: foundry type for hand composition, Linotype, and Monotype. Tschichold named his typeface for the famous Frankfurt typefounder Jacques Sabon (c. 1520–80).